# 'A' CUTE
## ANTHOLOGY

# 'A' CUTE
## ANTHOLOGY

### BY

### LYNN HARLE

Date of Publication:
June 2000


Published by:
Lynn Harle

Printed by:
ProPrint
Riverside Cottages
Old Great North Road
Stibbington
Peterborough
PE8 6LR

# CONTENTS

**And a Thank You to :-**

Brian & Margaret McSparron (Mam &Dad) Who held me
 together.

All my family & Friends Old & New Who gave me the
encouragement to keep going, especially Vanessa.

Austin & Maureen Who assisted with the production of this book.

1996.
1. FREEDOM!

Sometimes when we are ill and in despair
It's just as well hospitals like this one are there
So when you have been sectioned don't lose heart
People still love you even though you're apart
Look at this picture and what do you see?
A school of dolphins swimming free
We will always care no matter what you say or do
And very soon one of those dolphins will be you.




2. ROUTE TO RECOVERY
(ODE TO ANXIETY SUFFERERS)

Sit or lie peacefully
Listen to the water gurgling softly
Then close your eyes
And very soon you will realise
That you will come to no harm
So slow down to become calm

Take in a deep breath, lungs inflate
Breathe out with a sigh, deflate
Control each thought, breath and sensation
In order to feel relaxation
Imagine this picture to be reality
Share and enjoy its' tranquillity

Think of this rhyme
Concentrate for a time
A sinking feeling, simply rest
See this picture at its best
Colourful, beautiful, wonderful, look deep
Abide 'till almost asleep
Now slowly open your eyes
And to your surprise

You are no longer fearful or tearful
Instead feeling quite cheerful
At peace within
Yourself and nature akin.


## 3. SUNRISE, SUNSET

Sunrise and sunset
Have not yet met
And the journey in between
Must ALL be seen
A colourful and meaningful life
Will include pain and strife
But don't allow troubles to lie low
Into this radiant sky let them flow.


## 4. THE KINGFISHER

The Kingfisher, a bird of colourful array
Diving down to make the water spray
A fisherman of sort
Proud of what he's caught
Feeds the newly hatched
In a bank side nest, not thatched
Beauty begins
With these tiny things
Each one to grow
And in turn to dive to and fro
Plunging deep
Thoughts we suffer to keep
Can be brought to the surface
Like fishing, for a purpose
Trust and share
With those who care
Develop the beauty within
Let life begin.

## 5. LOVE

To have understanding and to care
About someone and how they fare
A very small word
That is NOT always HEARD
Honesty and of which
Is both pure and rich
Coming straight from the heart
Should be said from the start
Kindness and sweetness therein
Don't suppress, speak out, whether of FRIEND of KIN.


## 6. STIGMA

The terms used in diagnosing mental illnesses we find
Sound very unkind
And with what some people hear
There comes this fear
An ignorance which seems widely caught
Held fast without giving real thought
This on the whole is very unfair
Thank ........... there are those who do care!


## 7. THOUGHTS AND FEELINGS

Thoughts, all in a muddle
In need of a cuddle
Find a quiet place
Let those thought race
Spend time
To write a rhyme

Feelings, anger and hatred so deep
Why do we keep?
Failing to shout
Yet raging to be out
Talk a while with staff
In a story, end of paragraph.

## 8. RELEIVING TEMPER OVER STIGMA

For wounds to heal, first anoint
Be sharp, to the point
The power of speech
With reason to reach
Direct an  image, oneself Impress
Everyone has the RIGHT to express.

## 9. FRIENDSHIP

Friendship is just being there
Not only in despair
To enjoy each others company
Like singing in harmony
Music of laughter fills the air
Sunlight beams, eyes aglare
Brightened by future joys and hopes
Of contact, caring of how each other copes.

## 10. FLIPPING

A common term I use for relapse
My mood swings being vivid
Lack of sleep and back-up medication
Attack and almost close the eyelid

Concentrate, I must concentrate on conversation
But my attention is given to echoing voices
Mostly I hear my name repeated over and over
I hear laughing, yet no-one rejoices
I want to get up and leave
But am afraid, to hurt or offend
It takes courage to seek support, finally
Once given, then understood, these wicked noises I need no
longer contend.

## 11. TO THE ABUSER FROM THE ABUSED
## (CHILD, NOW IN ADULTHOOD)

You were trusted
How could you have abused that trust?
A child who easily gave love
Yet received none when there was a must!

Emotional damage, dark shadows of grey
I felt enclosed in a dim room on a bright Summers' day
Physical or sexual hurt, whichever
Should be a never, NEVER!

I cannot understand you
What did I do wrong?
My burning rage causes me to self-harm
YOU should be punished by a throng!!

## 12. WARD TROLLEY PHONE

A very important device
Sometimes the only means of communication
We seek support and advice
A source of information

We seek comfort too
ALL patients do
Like being kissed
When not in use is sadly missed.


## 13. UNDERSTANDING

Do you understand what I am telling you?
Can you relate to things that I've been put through?
The pain, the fear, the anger, sometimes I feel like I've had enough
No-one receiving such a rough time could be so tough
Give me a knife and I would wildly stab at the heart!
I would even, with my bare hands, rip it apart!!
To protect others they should have on their forehead a brand
Now, do you understand?
Thank heavens, you do?
Thank you, thank you, God bless, I found you.


## 14. LOCKED DOORS

The heavy door closes the noise of which echoes
Standing, staring out, feet are froze
To the long corridor floor of freshly cleaned tiles
If the door was opened again those feet would run for miles
A sigh, false smile and a good-bye wave
Disappointment hidden within, for freedom we crave
The truth we know, that it's for the best
But the feelings for being LET OUT are there, whether we are on
the go or we rest.

## 15. MY SILLY LYRIC

The elephant is a funny bird
It jumps from bough to bough
Builds its' nest in a rhubarb tree
And whistles like a cow

This silly verse was told to me, and I told it to a friend so dear
This friend, since school days , I have not seen in many a year
But this silly lyric reminds me of her and the happy side of my
childhood
So when feeling down and dwelling on bad memories, flick
through your past for something good.

## 16. DELAVAL WARD

A place of sanctuary, but not to hide
A place of friendship, where people are thoughtful and kind
A place to share our burdens, held deep inside
A place to receive help, the feeling of security we find.

## 17. STAR OF BETHLEHEM

On a table in the corner of the observation room
Stood a plant in full bloom
The Star of Bethlehem was its' name
"The Colour Purple", but from whence it came?

It was indeed a kind gesture
The reason for which only the owner knew
But kinder still was for the person to share this beautiful piece
of nature
So in turn this poem could be written from me to you.

## 18. HOPE

I hope to find some meaning in life
No meaning, no hope, what is there left?
Comfort me, help me gain the strength
Taken from me, the result of a terrible theft

Hold me close
Don't ever let me go
I'll take whatever dose
So that cold winds never blow.

## 19. A PLATE OF SALAD

Colourful food upon my plate
Tastier fruit and vegetables I never ate
Staying healthy in body, what of soul?
I'M STATING my aim and my internal goal
Give me good reason
And like the food in season
I will grow healthy in mind once more
Thoughts and feelings corrected, tears no longer pour.

## 20. ANNS' SOCKS

Jazzy socks brighten our day
A splash of colour comes walking your way
"Please hurry and wash them"we say
Not just for the smell, but to make us feel gay.

## 21. NOTICEBOARD

A source of information about things we need to know
It's especially nice to read of who's to come and go
Activities to do, the time of which are told
Headings that catch the eye are printed in bold.


## 22. TREES

Swaying back and forth in the wind with a rustle
Branches, twigs and leaves like busy shoppers in a bustle
Colours of green, brown and red all in a mix
To the earth God meant you to stay, affix
Why then do we cut you down?
To drop upon ground, ploughed and earthy brown
We should protect, not end a life
Give you the kind of break, like a holiday in Fife!


## 23. CARS

A wonderful way to get around
Looks are great and the engine has a lovely sound
But a killing machine is what it can be
Alcohol - compare it to drowning in the sea
So, when out drinking in a club, or pub, or even at home

Remember there are OTHERS about, including dogs, and cats
that roam.

## 24. THE CLOCK ON THE WALL

Time flies when we are having fun
Or soaking up the Summer sun
However, it seems to stop when we are low and dwell
We keep on looking at the clock because we can't tell
It also stands still when we look forward in anticipation
And this is so for all the nation.


## 25. ON DUNCAN GRAY

A wonderful man
Who will do anything for you he can
A man of great talent
But often too silent
Kind, caring and considerate
His friendship, its' worth, consolidate.


## 26. MUSIC

Music like emotions can run high
Whether in sound or pitch like birds in the sky
An octave or two lower
Perhaps even slower
Eventually silence takes over
But soon we recover
Beginning anew
Like a new house with a new view.

## 27. RAGE

Inner rage, a burning fire
Giving us a wrong desire
Lashing out at objects there
Hoping that it will clear the air
Lashing out at other people seems thoughtless
Even lack of self-control somewhat careless
But reasons behind the actions are sought
And with help these can be fought.


## 28. THE CHAIR

Sitting there
In front of a window, on the chair
Was the man
Hidden, tears ran
This sudden "flashback"
At night, in the black
A fear, the want to scream
The sudden remembrance, in a dream
Tear out this sight
See me through this plight
I'll talk to release the pressure
Please help me in my venture.

## 29. HOT CHOCOLATE

A cup and a saucer, inside delight
But the milk bubbled over, try as I might!
Oh, how it went to town
However when it cooled down
Half of my drink was gone
But I suppose that half a cup's better than none.

Inspired by Vanessa & Kevin.

## 30. DREAMS

My head hits the pillow
Where do I go?
I fall asleep
Sink into my dreams deep
Toss and turn all night
Scream out and fight
Awake in the morning
Thankful for the sun, and a new day dawning.

## 31. CONSTANT OBSERVATION

A watchful eye
I'm on constant
Each movement I make
To keep control, important

My freedom, therefore, is a miss
The thought of this gain, is a bliss
If I do lose control it's not my fault
Help me through 'till I come to a halt

Tell me that it will come to an end
So I may describe a better me, in letters I send
Meanwhile keep watch, in you I trust
As when in starvation, you are the crust.


## 32. POOL

Pool can be a game of laughs
From the onset of the break
Line up, angle right and into the pocket
SOME people make it seem like a piece of cake!

Inspired by Lee.


## 33. MY UNTOLD MEMORY

I am a child alone in the dark
Not allowed my seat to park
Made to stand so stiff, my body to ache
Crying for someone to " help me!" for goodness sake
I am shivering now, on landing so cold
All is secretive, and still untold
Now, God give me strength to carry on
My help I've found in speech, verse and song.


## 34. THANK YOU

Thank you for the flowers that grow
And everything in the world below
Thank you for the birds that sing
And the sunshine of the Spring.

I wrote this verse as a child
Now I'm grown and remembering past times
Some happy, but mostly sad, memories mixed
I sincerely hope to help others through my rhymes.


## 35. E.C.T.

In conversation, static electricity
Reminded me of E.C.T.
The results of which are good
But the treatment, often not understood
To the public perhaps more should be explained
Then understanding WOULD be gained.

Inspired by Michael (Nurse).


## 36. FAITH

In God we trust
But when we are thrust
Into situations of hurt
Like falling into a pile of dirt
We often lose faith in God and all
And need that "Come on, all you need do is call"
A few words from the bible, the aim, we never again shall fall.

## 37. STAPLES

My wound is held together
To heal the external, endeavour
But to heal the outside, first heal within
I am clean, free of sin.


## 38. DICTIONARY

Voices in the corridor
I hear them all day long
My thoughts , my actions always repeated
Misunderstood, totally wrong!

(I was upset when I wrote this verse, and looking up words in a
dictionary probably for the game of scrabble must have upset me).


## 39. SNORING

I could hear your snoring
Vibrations through the floor
So much so that eventually
I had to close every door!

Inspired by Vanessa & Michael (Patient).


## 40. SEEKING ATTENTION

Attention we seek
When inside we are weak
At anything and everything we strike out
And needing help is not in doubt.

## 41. A SINGLE CARD

A single card
Sweetness shown
Takes me from the hard
To kindness known
Give me that card any day
Show me love and lead the way.

## 42. SILENCE

Sitting in silence
Voices are quiet, excellence
Or "Quieter" should I say
They never seem to go away
They have led to "Ending of life"
Something, someone is missing, no longer a wife
My children I think of playing around
There joyous games and laughter upon the paved ground
Some day I'll look back when full of dismay
Remembering, the sun doth shine the warmest ray.

## 43. FEAR

What do I fear?
Why break out in a cold sweat?
Is it in my nature
When I'm under threat?
But experienced people tell me EVERYONE does so
And, perhaps I'll find it easier to relax, now that I know.

## 44. MEDICATION

My medication helps me through
Its' aim to stop me from feeling blue
If I think of an image, of a rainbow
Each colour stepping up from the one that's below
Then I can visualise a journey
Perhaps like flying from here to Turkey
I'll give you a wave when I reach that stair landing
I've conquered, forgot all my malhandling.

## 45. ENCOURAGEMENT

The encouragement I needed , you have given to me
And the interest you have shown, has refreshed like a cup of
tea
Inspiration has come from the source
Other reactions I will perceive in due course
But in all honesty
You have perhaps made a book reality.

Dedicated and Inspired by Karen.

## 46. A HANDBAG

A handbag I carry around
And when I sit down I put it on the ground
It is always with me wherever I go
And if it's not there I miss it so
Reaching down thinking it was there
And forever grasping at thin air
So when at last I have it, I'm happy
And once again I am "At the ready!"

## 47. SPEAKING OUT

Speak out, speak out
If need be, then shout
What is said is BETTER out, than in
We don't mind if you create a din.

## 48. MY DOORBELL

My doorbell never rings
Because it is broken so it seems
But I say "It's just one of those things"
When my visitors get wet, when it teams
"You should have knocked", I always repeat
While they are still wiping their feet
"We forgot!" they often say
But it does keep unwelcome visitors away!

## 49. APATHY

"Am I without feeling?" I hear you say
When along the corridor a fair way
I stopped, sank to the floor to think
Don't you analyse every blink!
Sometimes feelings, for whatever reason, we need to hold back
But it does not mean there is a lack!

## 50. PSYCHOSIS

My Psychosis has begun
Once more the web is spun
A tangled mess alone I hang
Awaiting my illnesses hunger pang
Is there no escape?
A way, a door agape
When I seek solitude and cry to myself
Be my helper, like pixie and elf.


## 51. FLARE

Send up the flare
I'm in distress
Make someone aware
Of this heartlessness
Make me a cover
Which back I can fold
Befriend another
One more hand to hold.


## 52. PROTECT

Protect your own
Show them the love that you were never shown
Get to know them very well
So to YOU, EVERYTHING they will tell.

## 53. SAUSAGES AND BEEFBURGERS

Give me a pork sausage every day
Cook it in whatever way
Looking tasty on my plate
Hunger pangs, no longer wait

Give me a beefburger often too
As you nearly always do
Not too much, mind
As I've heard said, "'Lest I reach around to lick my behind!"

## 54. OBSESSION I (TIDINESS)

Repeat! Repeat!
Everything kept so nice
Neat! Neat!
Don't even think twice
Have you heard of my plight?
How do I stop?
Show me how to put up a fight
Before my mind causes my body to drop.

## 55. NATURE CALLS

Tinkle, tinkle, as we do
While hovering over a strange loo
NATURE CALLS, so as we do
Give a sigh of relief, then TALLY-HOO!
Then oh no, not again
I'm worse than the British Rain!

## 56. ACCEPTANCE

Accepting an illness is half the battle
Problems then, you can tackle
"Amazing Grace"
Describes this place
A need is there
I'm now aware
Before, I was lost
Misunderstood, to the side tossed
Now, I am found
In BOTH mind and body, sound.


## 57. OBSESSION VII (POETRY)

When I awoke I knew, then I heard
Created poetry in my dreams, this is not absurd
Obsessiveness is the reason
My illness is therefore in season
My mind, it does not rest
And produces results of my best.


## 58. RHYMING

How do I keep SOME thoughts at bay
Because they always get in the way
Please teach me prose, Duncan Gray
Gently, let the rhyming fade away

I will listen to everything you say
I will put into practice, so obey
We will have to meet up, one day
At Ardgowan, through patio door, a sunny ray.

## 59. ORPHAN

When we feel safe
What are we like?
No longer a waif
Not in that familiar dyke
Give me a home
Somebody please read this poem
Love me with all your heart
And I'll show my gratitude, 'been rescued from the mart.

## 60. NATURE

A beautiful morning in late Spring
Summer is almost here, the birds, they sing
Paired up in trees and hedgerows with offspring
What a pleasant, soothing feeling nature can bring.

## 61. HOLIDAY

I long for a holiday
I see planes fly overhead on their way
If in luck, maybe one day soon
But it's much more likely to be stepping on the moon
I'd love a break
AND someone to take
It's no fun being on your own
Anyway, I can't afford the loan.

## 62. BIN

Full of rubbish, and oh how they stink
From milk cartons to fishy tins, what will the neighbours think
So next time you throw out cat litter, paper or rag
Remember first, to seal it in a bag!

## 63. SURPRISE

I am a dizzy blonde
I never get things right
And when (from behind) Des puts his arms around me
I often get a fright!

## 64. A HOLE IN THE WALL

When there is only one brick missing
The hole can easily be patched up
But, when there are many gone
I end up throwing a cup

One by one they must be put back
With cement, like nail, to tack
It may never reach being complete again
But life will go on once more, now that I'm sane.

## 65. NURSERY RHYMES

These rhyming verses
Meanings of which the years have outgrew
Many books contain the old ones
Never some that're new
Wouldn't you think someone would write maybe just a few
With simple meanings and easy words
Like "Once upon a time", people all knew
A story or tale, with joys to be shared
All so nice and forever true
You might try, give it a thought
This may be your cue, a different point of view.

## 66. SLEEPLESSNESS

At night I cannot sleep
I want to sink into slumber deep
I drink a cup of tea or coffee
In the hope that pleasant dreams I will see
Unknown to me I eventually doze
When I awake I am absolutely froze
Then I go to bed at last
Hoping to forget the past
Into this routine I have become used
And have ended up tired and all confused
With my problems I WILL come face to face
I have made up my mind, I am in the right place.

Inspired by Hazel.

## 67. PAST REGRETS

At school in the yard I would play
And when the Dinner Lady asked "What do you want to be?"
I'd say
"A doctor is what I want to be"
But alas this was not meant for me
Instead I became a wife
And led a completely different life
But through my tears and all my sorrow and heartache
Perhaps I've found my vocation, for others' sake.


## 68. OBSESSION II (WASHING)

I feel like dirt
And if I seem curt
Perhaps then I should explain
Your sympathy and understanding to gain
I wash myself over and over each day
In the hope that in this way
My memories can be washed away, clean
That they no longer can be seen.


## 69. LIFE IS A BITCH

Why are some people cruel?
I am not hardened, like thickened gruel
Wicked words and deeds penetrate
I am breaking down at a fast rate
Mend you ways!
And this craze!
Please can we live in harmony
For at the moment "Life is a bitch!", an eternity.

Inspired by Nora

## 70. RADIATOR

Warmth you give to me
But cost the earth to run, it's never free
However on cold Winter nights
I can relax, and throw aside those extra pair of tights!

## 71. A DAY IN THE COUNTRYSIDE

I travel far away from towns and cities
From crowds of people and chip butties
To the peace and quiet of the countryside
Where wildlife in abundance hide
But if you stay quiet enough you might see
A fox, weasel or stoat, to name but three
This calms the inner self we feel
And this in turn begins to heal.

## 72. A PAIR OF PIGEONS

On the grass and at the door they wait
Someone has been feeding them of late
Together they search for food we never ate
And their chicks are getting fatter at a steady rate!

## 73. AN EMBRACE

An embrace, happiness expressed
When greeting one another, brother and sisters' love confessed
Do this plenty
Life is no longer empty
Show your feelings, the truth within
You are close to me, my dearest of kin.

Inspired by Vanessa & Kevin.

## 74. VIOLENCE

Of violence I am afraid
From the depths within there is a rage
Explosions as on a bombing raid
Held back, locked inside a cage
If ever it gets out
I won't be able to help myself
So don't scream or shout
Please keep whatever it is to yourself.

## 75. A DECISION I HAD TO MAKE

Once I was asked to write some poetry
Its' content of which I was not sure
I made it straight to the point
The lines somewhat fewer
I did not agree with what was said
But it was exactly what rang in their head
I hope this did not bring upset
Or cause an act of violence to onset.

## 76. REMEMBERING IAN

Do you remember the day, I tried to run away
I wasn't very happy and I didn't want to stay
I kicked off slippers whilst heading on my way out
And all I heard was somebody, after me, shout
Across the grass with another nurse, you chased after me
When half way along you slipped and hurt you knee
But catching me wouldn't have mattered in any case
I could go NO FURTHER, 'cos I was out of breath and red in face!

Inspired by Ian (Nurse)


## 77. MY FEAR UPSETS ME

I need to rest
That would be for the best
But if I lose concentration
Someone would be on my mind, infiltration
I'm now afraid to be with them on my own
The fears people have passed on, firmly sown
I cannot sit in a room with that person
I wish there could be a different version.

## 78. BUTTERFLIES

Butterflies in my stomach, not the kind of sort
We would like to have on our mind for a thought
On a better note I'd like to say "Calmness"
Think of Gods small creature, fluttering to flowers in all
eagerness
Colourfully marked, and notice it we ought
It gives us lots of pleasure even though its' life is short
"Stillness in my stomach" now I say
Think of THE BUTTERFLIES in the garden, and settle down
in this way.


## 79.  MORE THAN MY FILL!

Pestering voices will persist
Trying not to hear, to worsen resist
There are people around me and T.V. too
Should I stay or leave, what should I do?
While I am writing they seem to fade
Yet I can't forget the noise they made
Hoping they'll quieten further still
I've had enough, more than my fill!


## 80. WORRIES

I hope she did not take offence
Take a step back in defence
The poem was meant to please
A pretty picture I could have painted with ease.

Written after giving "The Star of Bethlehem" to Dawn.

## 81. INSENSITIVE

Some things you say are so insensitive
When all I am doing is trying to be creative
For you my pictures aren't any good
My poems not read, so not understood
Don't you have a civil tongue!
Perhaps in it I should stick a bung!


## 82. RELIEVING TENSION

"Relieving tension"
Was my intention
And in return, what you said was nice to hear
The words so expressive and sincere.


## 83. THE CHANGE OF LIFE (MENOPAUSE)

When the weather is cold, I feel hot
The flushes come over me rather a lot
They also happen when least expected
AND to other people, so commented
But the worst time for me is when in my bed
I'm soaked in sweat from toe to head
I wish that these hot flushes were through
So I can do many more things, and sleep the whole night too!

Inspired by Anne.

## 84. CAR CHASE (T.V.)

A T.V. car chase reminded me
Of panic attacks, in mind still vivid, you see
I could not stand a lot of loud noise around then
And turned down the T.V. more than often.

## 85. MY BEDROOM

My bedroom, my sanctuary
A place secretive and images produced imaginary
Religious for a time, but that one time went
Because many hours of unanswered praying I had spent
Everyone seemed to have abandoned me
I wasn't transparent so they could not see
When I look back it's from that outside
I no longer wish to run, and to hide.

## 86. OBJECTS

It is strange that many objects have reminded me
Of thoughts and feelings, and produced, poems for all to see
It would have been better to show a reflected image
NOT a realistic view, but to onlook, envisage.

## 87. MY POEMS

I'd like to share my poems with you
But only if you would like me to
The words are personal, not all nice
And they mean a lot to some, like a bowl of rice
People who relate
To these word can celebrate
Those who do NOT
Will very soon have forgot.

## 88. HARD BUTTER

I wanted to put butter on my toast
The place being warm, leaves it melted like the grease of a
Sunday  roast
But this time I was taken by complete surprise
It was hard, and with my knife stuck in, it still would not prise.

Inspired by Vanessa.

## 89. KICK-BOXING IN THE CORRIDOR

He is Kick-boxing in the corridor
Feet athudding on the floor
He also practises on trees
Because, take cover, everyone flees!

Inspired by Tony.

## 90. DRAWINGS

In different mediums we recreate
Drawings of subjects, we hold great
And often to catch the eye of another
We add a little splash of colour.

## 91. SMOKING

Why inhale that rotten stuff
Pack them in you've had enough
Giving up is not so tough
It's better than wheezing and feeling rough!

Inspired by Vanessa

## 92. ON VANESSA

In Vanessa's company I am most calm
Taken away is the feeling of alarm
And the thought of self-harm
Friendship valued, as in handshake palm to palm.

## 93. TO LET YOU KNOW HOW I PHYSICALLY FEEL, I.

I feel a cold coming on
I can hardly breathe the air I thrive upon
This is ALL I need at this time!
I thought I'd tell you in a rhyme.

## 94. TO TELL YOU HOW I PHYSICALLY FEEL, II.

My body is rapidly getting tired
My eyes are heavy and have almost retired
I had some sleep though last night
So my mind has rested some, and my thoughts and feelings are
quite light.


## 95.  THANK YOU II.

Thank you for the time you spared
To show how much you really cared
Your  support was greatly needed
This poem, to say that it was gratefully appreciated.

Written for Vanessa & Karen.


## 96. LISTENING

I am listening all the time
To take my mind off it I make up a rhyme
Do people think I am made up of concrete?
This lack of feeling makes life incomplete!


## 97. BIRDS

So many birds fill the skies
Far above the hilltops they rise
In valleys and dales we often see
So many different breeds flying free
Should we also live in harmony?
Do you, with me, agree.

## 98. I AM PSYCHIC

I believe I am Psychic
For me, something of great importance
Give me the gift to know about each antic
And help others with more confidence.

## 99. LOSS OF CONFIDENCE

Withdrawing, seeking solitude
Often over someone else's attitude
Nasty things which have happened, day and night consume
on which we dwell, alone, in a darkened room.

## 100. SUDDEN REMEMBRANCE

Pieces of glass I remembered
And this I linked with poetry rendered
With sudden remembrances like this I am fascinated
But welcome is the knowledge of how the two are related.

## 101. THE FOX (4.30 a.m.)

At early morning the sweet harmony of nature does ring
Hear the peacefulness of the birds that sing
A lone red fox over the greenness silently went
Hunting for rabbits as nature meant
As nature meant, as clear as that day
Survival, is the way.

## 102. THE OWL

The hoot of the owl in content
Feeding its' young with what nature sent
At night, swooping down silently upon its' prey
With dark eyes tightly shut during the day
God bless this swift hunter and its' offspring
And let there be plentiful of what it needs to bring.

Dedicated to Aunty Peggy.

## 103. A TREE

A tree
Is it a pillar in society?
Hands outreaching to embrace
Fingers touch, but leaving no trace
We grow them to cut down, what a disgrace!
Just to wipe our backsides, hands and face!!

## 104. HAMSTER

Coffee is her name
And she's really very tame
You should see her latest craze
That is, whizzing through her maze!

Written for Mark & Kevin.

## 105. PICTURES HANGING ON THE WALL

There's many a picture hanging on the walls
From pretty flowers to fox hunting calls
But what is really getting to me of late
Is that there's not one hung up blooming well straight!


## 106. SCRABBLE

The game of scrabble we like to play
Each and every single day
But to catch LEE you have to get up with the larks
And to make it even harder, the score he marks!


## 107. A BOWL OF SUGAR

Sweetness, sweetness
One spoonful or two
Yes, please do
But mind the brown lumps now, 'cos there's a few!


## 108. DES'S FLOOR

With mop and bucket off he goes
Watch your step and mind your toes
Give us a wave when you're done
Then spilling our tea cups, down the corridor we run!

## 109. TEA BAG

Out with a cup then we make our tea
Stir it around 'till colour we see
Then, we mast it for a minute
Now we leave our soggy tea bag, don't even bin it!

## 110. MILK

At breakfast time there is milk in plenty
But come supper time the jugs are empty
And all the culprits have flown
So find a cow and milk your own!

## 111. BLEEPER

A bleeper from Otterburn, it was lost
The nurses, they could not find it at any cost
Because unknown to them it had sank
To the bottom of Delaval's fish tank!

## 112. COFFEE

I made myself a cup of coffee
A change from making tea
And when I saw a piece of crayon that was toxic
I felt an urge to retch, that's be sick!

## 113. WATER FIGHT

Vanessa and I threw my slippers at each other
And when we were fed up with that, moved on to water
At first, a little we flicked, and then more
Until finally, we'd flooded the kitchen floor!


## 114. VANESSAS' PIT II

VANESSAS' bed is called her pit
That's because she is always in it
But one morning Bev sorted her out
Because sheets, quilt and mattress she was left without!
She'd pulled the lot off!!


## 115. SIZE 14's

I bought a pair of size 14 trousers
And had to fit in them with a shoe horn, to push in my tum
But when I walked down the corridor
I lost my knickers up the crack of my bum!


## 116. FALLING DOWN

I went chasing after my Nephew
When a stumbling I did go
Made a crater in the ground
And said "Oh my poor elbow" (And the rest!)

## 117. A WOBBLY TABLE

In the dining room there is a table
That is definitely not very stable
Under one leg we should stick somebody's' cap
So your dinner doesn't end up in your lap.

## 118. MY FLASHBACKS

Flashbacks fascinate me, a weird sort of dream
Yet so uncontrollably cold they also seem
Thoughts, sounds or smells can induce
To fight them is of no use
A vivid picture from a buried past
Brought forth, at last
As a child it was an attempt to forget
That we did not tell there is a regret
But now that it's out it can be dealt with
No longer sink into an imaginary world, a myth
When the pieces are fitted together and locked tight
A better life we shall lead, for what we KNOW has been put
right
The pain and the hurt we can throw aside
Be calmer and more at peace with the world, inside
At the end of the day, we have grown stronger
For flashbacks we no longer hunger
The story as it was, has been told in full
Looking forward, life appears no longer dull
Because the wild frenzy of rage has gone
And self-harm is no longer done.

Dedicated to Karen and Dawn.

## 119. SELF-HARM

A compulsive wave keeps coming over us to self-harm
The wave, inner rage, breaks up the calm
Like a stormy sea at full tide
We must talk ourselves out of it, 'till that tide subsides
Seek out help from those we TRUST
Having faith in others is a MUST
Let the difficult times flow pass
Far from that sea, float down a mountain stream, bad thoughts
surpass.

Dedicated to Karen and Dawn

## 120. CALM

The wave has left me now
I may wipe the sweat from my brow
The tears are drying on my face
Even under nose and chin, not a dry place
I didn't really want to do it
My heart was never actually in it
And my wounds I know will heal
Although scars for life I can reveal
Like those inside, too
I pray to God to pull me through
The tide, yet again
Until the spray hits me in the face, like rain
One wave after another attacks me
'Till at last, the storm has passed leaving a calmer sea
Low tide, and calmer still
No longer a need to take that relaxing pill
Absorb the beauty around you, today
Feel the harmony of mind and body, this way
Set free of the bad, good times will come fast
Sail through easier each time, until content at last.
(Dedicated to Karen and Dawn.)

## 121. THE BIFFA BIN

A Biffa bin was outside standing
And the wind had blown the lid back
Down came Rooks, Jackdaw, Magpie and Pigeons landing
And ripped open the plastic bag of black
For me, they could eat what was inside, I must confess
But the daft birds created one heck of a mess!

## 122. HELLO / GOODBYE

I said Hello when I really meant Goodbye
I didn't like them one bit, I cannot tell a lie
I would rather find floating in my soup a fly
Or have sore and itchy eyes because of a sty!!

## 123. THE HOLE IN THE WALL II

Mended, that hole in the wall
Bricks stuck solid, none shall fall
A wall complete
No longer repeat
From here grow stronger
Ever taller, ever longer
Never weak, or rocky
Ever more strong and plucky
Once more, myself.

## 124. RAIN

Standing, staring into space
Wishing we could be in some other place
The pitter patter of the rain
The trickling of water going down the drain
When God is sad
His tears wash away the bad
"Cease", the rain
"Happiness", once again.


## 125. MOUNTAIN STREAM

How sweet is the sound of the water that flows
How melodic when also the breeze blows
Mountain stream
A Summers' dream
Nature and me
In harmony.


## 126. THE SPIDER PLANT

Many leaves of green and white
Hanging over pot, so light
Like tiny fingers of a baby reaching out
The young spider plant growing about
On arms so long
But also strong
A beautiful Sight
To it, the memory, hold on tight.

## 127. GROUP ACTIVITY

Everyone doing their activities
Quiet, peaceful, concentration
Then it's time for tea and coffees
And everyone gathers around in a circle, congregation
Pleasant conversation of things that they have done
Of mixed topics, mingled together
Then people leave one by one
Happy with what they have created and ACHIEVED,
ALTOGETHER.

Dedicated to the staff of the Occupational Therapy Department.

## 128. SPECIAL WORDS - IRENE

Someone so kind and caring
Was taken so quickly from us
No pain was felt, forbearing
To bring her back, a fuss
But alas to no avail, her life had faded away
She passed on, this day
Words of love cannot be expressed
For weeks we had not seen each other
Words of love should have been confessed
But neither of us did bother
Yet, I'm sure she knew, deep down, how much she meant to me
Now in spirit, watching over us, but of pain free.

## 129. KAREN

With a stroke of my hand over her forehead
Letting her know how much I care
Waiting until she has fallen asleep
Wishing her sweet dreams, somewhere
Far from the memories of badness
No amount of alcohol can produce long-lasting happiness
Never to fall back into that trap
Rest now, begin again, after this nap
May God Bless You.


## 130. KAREN II

I once knew someone who was desperate for a baby
Around her, friends and relatives had a family
She longed for a family of her own, constantly
But until she stopped harming herself this was out of the
question, definitely
Fighting with herself all of the time
Wrestling with loved ones and carers, sometimes
But with Gods' help, strength to pull through will be found
Then will follow a family, success, everything so sound.

## 131. AN EMPTY FRUITBOWL

Empty, empty
No more in plenty
Wasting away
From day to day
Poverty strikes
Not even push-bikes
Dry, sandy soil
No water to boil
Where is hope
No cleansing, no soap
How do they survive?
How desperate the need to thrive!
When your fruit bowl is full
Be forever thankful.

Written for people who are not eating properly, or have an
eating disorder.

## 132. OCCUPATIONAL THERAPY ROOM

A room full of various materials
Of poetry, art, gardening and other sorts of crafts
Pictures hanging on the walls
With display cabinets and filled shelves there too
Plenty of things to create here
To soft music, relaxing in fact
The idea, to relax and enjoy
To mix with others again, with calm mind and steady hands
To be sure of ourselves
Gaining back our self-confidence.

### 133. WINDMILL (O.T.)

A wooden windmill stands on a table
Painted deep colours of red, blue and white
With arms out-stretched, but still
Awaiting the first breath of wind
That will send them spinning as if ready to take flight
If it were not for the fact that they are fixed
Because THIS windmill is really a bird-box.


### 134. MOBILE (O.T.)

Large bright orange round sun of papier mache
With petals of blazing red light around it
Hanging from this sun are stars of yellow and orange
A brilliant splash of colour that would brighten up any pair of
eyes
Particularly a child's, but essentially those which have
saddened.


### 135.  BOWLS

It's competition time once more
Therefore the heavens open, and down pours the rain
And we play and play, but still the rain does not pass
Now we need a Vax to soak up the water from the grass.

## 136. VANESSA DOING A RUNNER

Vanessa hovered around in waiting
And when the opportunity arose she kicked off running
Elaine and Fiona followed in hot pursuit, then Des ran too
With Fiona shouting her normal "I'll deck you!"


## 137. CHAIRS IN OBS.

In Obs. we spend a lot of time sitting
Some of us get out cards, scrabble or knitting
But always when we sit down in the chairs for whatever,
perhaps even a smoke
They let out a noise like a Whoopee Cushion, a huge joke!


## 138. MY PRAYER

Dear God, please hear what I have to say
We all need to be comforted this day
A day when tears show our sadness
But there is also a hidden gladness
In knowing that you will be looking after ......... from now on
Please welcome him / her / them with prayer and song.


## 139. ORANGES

I had a pair of oranges, bright in colour
I ate then both and I felt fuller
Next morning I had to do a runner
Then I was relieved, and so much emptier!

## 140. DIET COKE

Diet coke, a fizzy drink so nice
I buy it whatever the price
But it's a pity that some places water it down
Do they think that I'm a clown!

Dedicated to Kelly.


## 141. NATURE

Nature knows no clock
No hours, no minutes, all time is spent
Yet holds so much stock
It is all planned, because nature was sent

I waited for the lone fox to come by
Three times I waited, he was nowhere nigh
Jesus was denied three times too
Because first, there is something else to do

Let us say, the lady will be brought
A Spiritual world must be sought
God helps those who seek
Not those who dabble and peak

The gift has been given
I have been blessed
Through me Jesus has again risen
The world be addressed

I suffer not for myself
But for someone I care for
Like pixie and elf
One good deed followed by more

The end is pleasing
A result worth seeing
God give us the grace
We live in an amazing place.

## 142. MY POEM

"Cheesed off" should be the name of this rhyme
I've not been like this for some time
Let me bring you up-to-date
I've not been a happy chappy, of late
Unhappy, miserable, sad
A better life I once had
But a better one still must be there waiting
I am hoping, anticipating
I know it will come along soon for me
I can't wait to see, I'll be in ecstasy!   (Written for Sharon.)

## 143. BEING PSYCHIC / A MEDIUM

Something new and exciting is happening to me
Quite out of the normal, but for all to see
Doctors, Freud wants to share in the experience
But alas there is a blockage, too much of own beliefs,
interference
A second opinion I now seek to gain
Or an appeal case, a chance to explain
I will win, whichever way
To be of help at the end of the day.

## 144. SHOWING ME THE WAY

I am GODS' Disciple, Peter
And with the help of Jesus I am stronger
The lone red fox came by today
Because I needed to be shown the way
My heart felt elated, too much to hold down
I felt a blessing upon my crown
Peter is here, I know now
My love of nature, the reason how
Because I am Peter, I CAN heal
Through Poetry, Art and Music I can reveal
I was almost kept waiting too long
But now I can celebrate and burst into song.

## 145. HONEYSUCKLE

Sweet smelling fragrance like the sweetness we see
Receiving caresses from the honey bee
True love is sweeter, that will come to be
Heartache over, of pain FREE.

## 146. PHOBIA

An intense fear
A sudden shock to the system
When they appear
We wish to escape from them
Calm thoughts are needed
As they are all Gods' creatures
A prayer therefore rendered
And they can bring about pleasures.

## 147. HOSPITAL BEDS

On a hospital bed, the mattress is covered with plastic
This means that to it you always stick!
And when you get up, all you hear is a spring
Awakening everyone because it's somewhat deafening!!


## 148. PAIR OF ZEBRA FINCHES

Zebra Finches are their name
And to have a breeding pair is the game
But alas some people do not care
Because feeding them bread means we could lose that pair!!


## 149. ALL I HAVE LEFT

I would like to explain how I feel
To your good nature I appeal
I am so anxious and not content
Because of one persons' bad intent
Having trespassed and stolen from me once already
I am so afraid that they will come back and maybe
Take what possessions I have left at home
I hope that you understand how upset I feel through this poem.

Written for Sharon.

## 150. MY FEAR UPSETS ME II

I have an inner fear
The reason for which I am not clear
Meeting someone for the first time
Often feels like I'm committing a crime
Not sure of how their attitude will be
Not sure of their reaction towards me
God will help my fear subside
In him I will trust, AND with him abide.

## 151. MY POEM

I thought that army life had broken me
But now I know that it was meant to be
Too much violence was there
And I was left in despair
The demons I have felt and seen
Are of badness that has been
I am a Medium, one of the best
AND I can give power to the rest.

## 152. LEES' DREAM

One night, at home, I had a futuristic dream
So vivid the pictures did seem
I saw strange red birds and creatures being chopped up by machinery
And I knew that insects and birds would become as common as that of the grains of sand on the seashore
Life cycles sped up and everywhere was full of insects and spiders
While everybody-else went through the black hole
I found myself on a futuristic space station which was used for interplanetary communication
With my lucky coin I tried to get cigarettes from a machine
But when I tried to pull them out cigarettes dropped onto the floor, and as I picked them up
A woman then cried Help! Help! Help! He's stealing all the cigarettes!
So, I ran upstairs, and into another room I was pushed by my mate who believed in science
He asked me if I wanted a cup of tea or coffee when, he put on the floor a purple visor
"Do you know what this is?" he asked
And I said "Yes, it is the third eye"
Then he asked me "Do you know what it is used for?
"Communicating with the dead", was my reply
But the visor was only seen on dead bodies and not on living people
My mate then said "Did you see it?"
The probe, which I had not seen, had been a millionth of the way into the black hole when it exploded
The galaxy had given birth to planets and they were everywhere
Everybody was saved
And a population explosion thus made.

## 153. LIGHTNING

Sometimes all is not what it seems
No-one has made judgement, so deemed
Continue to Church, hold your faith firm
And come through this incarnage, all will not be as it once seemed.


## 154. THE TELEPHONE

A very useful gadget you know
But not everyone feels confident with it, so
Think of butterflies in the garden
And flowers in the garden of EDEN
Think calmness and stillness
Always positiveness
And this clever instrument
Can lead to achievement
That is, the message can be spoken
When inside, in spirit, you have awoken.


## 155. A TIGHTNESS

I am a very nervous person
Of places and people I am uncertain
I have my own home at the moment
But accommodation is for me, now meant
Alas sometimes I would rather be on my own
And a nervousness there, I wish I could have outgrown
As symptoms such as a tightness in my chest I feel
And a shaking of the hands and a jerking of the neck seem unreal
Yet I am sure that God is with me
And looks over me, HE is the KEY.

Written for Brenda.

## 156. UNCONQUERABLE!

I was competing in competition
When someone spiked me drink - total destruction!
From then on things got worse
And I'd like to tell you in this verse
I am on a section
Supposedly for my own protection
Certain drugs they say I use
But this is only an excuse
To prevent me from competing
All the world seems to be against me, and I'm bleeding
The ache of not enjoying my sport - unbearable
The want to get back into the fight - UNCONQUERABLE!

Written for Tony.


## 157. PATIENCE

Patience is a virtue
Something of which fills you
Remember Jesus and calmly say
"I am going to slow down by Prayer", this way.

Written for Carol (Patient).

## 158. MY POEM

The urge takes me to drown my sorrows
Like a rabbit, I am hidden in burrows
Travelling so deep
Yet even deeper they seem to go
When will they end?
I beg of it so
God grant me the strength to carry on
I will pray , YOU I will lean upon
If I can be of pain free
The Church will be for me
I am being drawn
A new light at the end of the tunnel, a new dawn.
Alcoholism.

## 159. BIRDS II

St. Peter, now I know how he felt
When all the birds flocked down to him
Akin with nature and all its' offspring
At peace within
A glorious picture for eyesight or lens
A perfect note, in sequence, and in harmony
A balance forthwith, and again
A melody.

## 160. OBSESSION VI (KLEPTOMANIA)

In the past I have been compelled to take other peoples'
possessions
Things which do not belong to me
This is one of my obsessions
Not a very proud part of me
But I met someone who offered me trust
To give back therefore a must
A bond, a friend for life
I am through all my heartache and strife.

## 161. MEETING YOU - BILL

Bare-footed and alone you walked
Across the grass where the lone fox had stalked
From room to room, and window to window I watched
My eyes on you, firmly attached
I felt compelled to go to you
Something which God made me do
I was like a woman possessed
And when I reached you, of my poetry I confessed
To my delight, you wrote too
My poems will be published through and through
So excited afterwards, I was left "on a high"
Knowing of future contact and that you will be nigh
A friendship that I will have for life, and hold dear
Of this I am sure, absolutely clear.

## 162. MY POEM - TOM

I met a Medium today
And through my own poem told of voices in my head, and in a
way
A bond was formed at that time
And I was asked to write a rhyme
We had hugged and a force had been felt
I felt then, that the right cards for me had been dealt
The voices will not cease but be sorted
This is THE direction, this is how I will be comforted
My many guides will come through, but not all in one go
My laughing and giggling constantly will be less, so
I will not feel like I'm "on a high" always
And to the Lord, I will praise.


## 163. ENVIOUS

What you have got
Is what I want for sure
What you have not
Is the only known cure
Why this is so
Makes me feel low
I would not say you brag
But you will never see ME in a rag!
"C'mon", I say "C'mon"
Let these bad thoughts be gone.

## 164. HYPOCHONDRIAC

I'm ill, I'm terribly ill
Can't rest, can't stay still
What if it's bad news?
Oh, it's not just a bruise
What if it's cancer?
I need an answer
I'll visit my Doctor
Or maybe the Rector
Let the pain be gone!
Help me someone!!

## 165. ADDICTION

I crave, and I crave
I feel a wave, a wave
I pace the floor
I am wanting more
I am all tensed up
I am thirsty for a cup
I rant and I rave
I crave, and I crave.

## 166. A ROOM LIKE A CELL

Why have I been put here?
Without any cheer
Why have I been put here?
The reason's not very clear
Bare white walls
No flower or leaf that falls
No wardrobe for hanging up our clothes
No window, the blinds are fixed shut
No contact, people have given up
No food, no drink, I'm wasting away
No energy, night or day
No bonding, my baby seems like it's not mine
I need no help, when I get home everything will be fine.

## 167. MY HURT

I did not mean for you to get into trouble
Now I'm left like a pile of rubble
Because of constant things you did and the noises you made
A hurt terribly behind that facade.

## 168. SELF-DESTRUCTIVE THOUGHTS

I am self-destructing
Often with no interrupting
I am never right
I am putting myself down, a sight
I am absolutely hopeless
I am totally worthless
I am helpless too
I am not liked, others I do
Give me a hug, give me a smacker
Tell me I am NOT an utter Knacker!

## 169. PARANOIA

I doubt myself, and others
Most of reality, smothers
I think the whole world is against me
I can hear it all, you see
I know it's all in my head
I know the truth, the lie is dead
But on and on the thoughts they roll
I'd like to prevent, simply seal in a bowl.


## 170. OBSESSION IV (SPENDING MONEY)

I am a spend thrift
To get an uplift
I cannot keep money in my pocket
I'm off to the shops like a rocket
A dress, delicacies, whatever I like
To carry them I need much more than a pushbike
Will I ever, the shop, be able to attend?
Without the uncontrollable urge to spend!


## 171. OBSESSION V (FEAR OF SPENDING)

Afraid to spend, that is me
Never going on a spending spree
In my savings box it goes
Each coin is counted, no-one knows
The need may come
I could want some
The bank is full
Yet life is dull
Save me for goodness sake
So to spend some, I need a break!

## 172. GAMBLING

Compulsive is the word
But I am secretive, and not heard
One bet, one coin leads to more
I'd like to win, to even up the score
I rarely do, that is a fact
And how can I keep myself and family intact
Difficult times upon myself I bring
I never whistle, I never sing
Hold me back, and back, and back ........
Do not let the cards against me stack.


## 173. COMPULSIVE LYING

Never the truth, always a lie
It does not matter who is nigh
I am hiding something of shame
And I have no-one else to blame
Sooner or later I'll be caught out
An argument will follow, shout after shout
But what the heck am I to do?
I suppose once I'm caught, I'll be through.


## 174. BITTERNESS

A bitter taste in my mouth
Like a bird I wish to fly South
Northward bound and colder still
Wait a minute I'll take that pill
I really find it hard to forget
And often wish I could see a Vet
This bitter feeling toward you
I cannot ever subdue
Give me a kick in the shins
Then forgive me of my sins.

## 175. INTOLERANCE / IRRITABILITY

I am fed up with you
Everything about you, and everything you do
When you sit down, I want to stand up
The cup is full, but it's also and empty cup
I cannot listen to you at all
I wish I was above you, 10 feet tall
Then I'd really tell you where to go
Dish it out well, a staggering blow
I know I shouldn't, I'm only annoyed
But I've just found out my pools coupon's void.


## 176. SAYING NO

Why can I never say no?
When all the time I mean it so
Whatever it is I always say yes
Wherever it is I must confess
This leads to my being used
Something which cannot be excused
Don't give me Hell
I am not well.


## 177. PANIC ATTACKS

Panic attacks are will named
They are also world-wide famed
A fear of a fear
That is always here
Tear them away, I pray
Give me a care-free day.

## 178. FEELING DEPRESSED

How sad I feel at this time
I've had my share of difficult times, which I cannot tell of in this
rhyme
How low I feel at this time
Sometimes it's almost like a pantomime
But with no laughing
Or happy dancing
Can I ever get back to reality?
Exactly that, normality!


## 179. FEELING PHYSICALLY SICK

Nausea, vomiting, what is it like?
It's a bit like being in a dyke
A heavy head, that gets heavier still
It's holding me down, I've had my fill
I must keep climbing forever up
When I've reached my tea cup I'll drink my first cup
Keep on going higher again
I won't be washed away by the rain.


## 180. SLEEPINESS

My eyes are heavy
I feel I will doze off at any minute
My eyes are heavier
And my sleep I'm sure could be infinite
This is not what I want to happen, now or ever
So come on, give me a shake LIKE needs the WEATHER.

## 181. ENERGY

I am lacking energy
I am in need of an energising pill
I am slowed right down
I am lacking the skill
To pull myself back to normal
To do what I always did
To pick myself up when I fall
To put back on the lid.


## 182. I'M SICK OF BEING HERE

I'm fed up of being here
I do not want to stay, yet I have no fear
I simply want to be back home
Amongst other people I do not wish to roam
But deep down I know it must be
Even though I keep thinking, this is not for me.

Written for Sheila (patient).


## 183. OBSESSION VIII - ACCIDENTS

Always checking after everything I do
Worried about accidents coming to
Engulf me, whether fire, flood or the like
I feel like alerting everyone through a mike
"Can I stop?", I am wearing out
"Please stop! again I want to shout
Always hoping this will cease
And inside I will feel more at peace.

## 184. ON JONAPA

Jonapa is her name
And I am sure she will be of world-wide fame
Her destiny will begin today
I will lead her, show her the way
Jonapa is the name of a flower
I can picture the beauty in a light April shower
Herself, she is of beauty and free of sin
Projecting calm and peace from within.


## 185. PLEASE DO NOT FORGET ME

I am still your mother
So, please do not forget
I love you from my heart
So, please do not forget
I miss my Grandchildren too
So, please do not forget
Please do not forget
So that you never REGRET.

Written for Nan.


## 186. TIMES PAST I

Two middle-aged ladies at Bamburgh stayed
And one night they were out late
When they were going to Waren Mill
And as they were going down the hill
They saw a "Coble" where the hill fell away
They saw it where high tide would have come to that day
And as they tried to slow down in the car
They found that before they'd got very far
Through the "Coble" they had went
A stranger tale has never been sent.

## 187. TIMES PAST II (BAMBURGH CASTLE)

One night a young boy who resided in the keep
Where he normally lay under the roof which was flat not steep
Was going up to the stair landing
When around the corner a LADY in a pink dress was walking
He also heard one night when in his bed
Footsteps which were overhead
From times past there is an air of dismay
A haunted castle is what this is today.


## 188. SELF-CONFIDENCE

Have confidence
No more fear or incompetence
You NEVER lacked the latter anyway
Do not go, stay

AGROPHOBIA
Do not run, do not hide
When you are outside
Never fade away
Do not go, stay

CLAUSTROPHOBIA
Do not run, do not hide
When you are inside
Never cower away
Do not go, stay

OVER EATING
Do not seek comfort by over eating
When bad thoughts you are keeping
Never look BACK over that day
Do not go, stay

UNDER EATING
Do not seek comfort by under eating
When bad thoughts are leaping
Never WILL for that day
Do not go, stay

GUILT
Do not feel that you are to blame
When your heart is still aflame
Never be afraid to say
Do not go, stay

DENYING EMOTIONAL FEELINGS
Do not pretend that you don't feel
When everything is real
Never stop yourself, JUST SAY
Do not go, stay.


189. "TWO MINUTES"

I need you
"Just wait two minutes"
Remind you I do
"Just wait two minutes"
How long is two minutes?!
About as long as the time BETWEEN my DAILY visits!!

## 190. YET

I achieved my highest of achievements yet
I found a way of stopping my self-harming, and yet
When I asked to see, to tell you, you were busy with something else, yet
I waited and waited and still you did not come, yet
Then I finally came to the conclusion that I was at the back of the list again, yet
I walked out, and self-harmed, the biggest shame yet
I'm still waiting to see you and I've not seen you yet.


## 191 SHARING

I would have loved to have had a sister
So to have things to share
She would also have been a good listener
And we would have made a perfect pair
Lynn and Claire are that perfect pair.


## 192. WH?!

Who was that?!
Maybe I'll remember in a while
What was that?!
Maybe I'll remember in a while
Where have I put it?!
Maybe I'll remember in a while
Why did I do that?!
Maybe I'll remember in a while
Who? What? Where? Why?
Oh, to hell with it WHEN I remember, it will be in STYLE!!

Dedicated to Bill, but written for all those who suffer with their short-term memory after E.C.T. It helps to carry a note pad and pen to jot important things down.

## 193. TRAPPED

I am trapped
I cannot break free
Why am I trapped?
How do I decree?

I constantly laugh
This I cannot prevent
Why do I laugh?
How do I lose my speech content?

I pace the floor
I can't stay in one place
Why do I pace the floor?
How do I show my face?

I am uncomfortable with people
My memories are too harsh
Why do I move away?
How do I sink into a marsh?

I hear the voices
They whiz around in my head
Why do I hear them?
WHEN will they be said?!

## 194. UP AND DOWN

Up and down the corridor I walk
My feet are never still
Up and down, no time to talk
I think I'm pretty ill
But people ask me how I feel
And "yes" to them I reply
Things inside me seem so real
But to those outside, I DENY.

Inspired by Eamonn.

71

## 195. OUT ON THE GRASS

A bright sunny morning and I walk out onto the grass
All the birds are chirping merrily and light thoughts I surpass
The sweet smelling grass has just been cut short
And lie on it I feel I ought
A Ladybird flies nigh
And the Butterflies flutter high
Flowers of Honeysuckle, Rhododendron, Azalea, Viola and
Bluebells grow
Now all we need is a gentle breeze to blow.


## 196. TEARS

Holding back the fears
Means holding back those tears
Sometimes for years and years

Like when we are in arrears
Listening to neighbours laughs and sneers
Sometimes for years and years

When a bad thought nears
We wait for those jeers
Sometimes for years and years

We lose our careers
And our heart is full of spears
Sometimes for years and years

SO, holding back the fears
Means holding back those tears
Sometimes for years and years.

## 197. ALIENS

A helicopter flew above
Something I would love to have drove
How many landing?
One, two or three
Why are they here?
Because there's quite a few to see
What are they going to do?
Fire! Fire! Fire!

## 198. MY LOVE

My love for you is oh so strong
I worship the ground you walk upon
With every hug and kiss, I want more
When sinking down upon the floor
To be with you, an addictive crave
To want you, a compulsive wave
Butterflies in my stomach I feel
E.C.T., and like an electric bell for me you ap'peal!

## 199. NO SLEEP!

Why won't you let me sleep?
Why won't you let me lie?
You wake me up from slumbers deep
And all I can do is sigh.

Why won't you let me sleep?
Why won't you let me lie?
In and out you always peep
When I don't want you nigh

Why won't you let me sleep?
Why won't you let me lie?
In my bed you always leap
And I feel that I could cry

Why won't you let me sleep?
Why can't you let me lie?
I wish another bed to keep
Before I wish to die.


## 200. "I'LL DO IT FOR YOU"

I feel I've hurt those I hold most dear
I've thought of nothing else this past year
My drunkenness has caused this harm
A cry for help, my alarm
I wish I could turn back the clock
But my mind is full and thoughts run amok
God grant me the strength, and pull me through
Tell each of my loved ones "I'll do it for YOU".

Written for Robert.


## 201. THE TIGER

Behind those eyes so deep
Are thoughts which you alone keep
Such a lonely life you lead
No trust in others, no-one to impede
But those eyes are somehow reaching out
As if they were about to shout
"Would it be for help?" we ask
For we are here to carry out that task.

## 202. FROM PHIL TO LISA

Dear Lisa I love you so much
I love everything about you, especially your touch
Of late I have done a great deal of wrong
Drink, drugs and spending are VERY wrong
But I am suffering inside
And as a result hurt those outside
This does not mean that I do not care
Simply that my feelings I cannot share
I would never leave you for another
I love both you and our daughter
You and Charlotte are mine for ever
And to show my feelings of love for you I will endeavour.

## 203. FRIDAY NIGHT

Please someone, hear of my plight
I live only for a Friday night
No alcohol do I consume
When with you in that room
Yet at the end of the night I run and I hide
As the memories and feelings of another reach out from inside
Once more another Friday night has gone passed
And I long for another to come around fast.

Written for George.

## 204. MY POEM

I have enough, coping with my own problems, do you hear?
When I am able, I will help you, never fear
But right now I need to be alone, to hide
Because my own thoughts and feelings are about to burst out
from inside
I have my own way of coping with this, you see
And especially to be of other peoples' problems, free!

Inspired by Paul.

## 205. ON "FOOTSTEPS IN THE SAND"

Please let me tell you this story in a rhyme
When I was about to get married for the second time
I was worried about whether my son would fit in happily
When I wrote the story "Footsteps in the Sand", sincerely
This day I was walking along the beach
When I lost my son David and my husband Phillip, out of reach
I rushed around the dunes looking
When I saw footsteps in the sand going for miles without
stopping
I was panicking inside in case they'd been hurt and were lying
somewhere
When I saw an Ambulance on the pier which in me sent up a
flare
My son was lying on a stretcher after hitting his head on rocks,
and I found
That my husband had carried him all that way, and everything
was now sound.

Written for Christine.

## 206. GLAD TO BE ALIVE

One cold, dark and windy night
Late night, no-one in sight
I came downstairs in my pyjamas only
Opened the door and walked over to the tree, standing solely
The wind was around the tree swirling
And picking up leaves which were around it lying
I sat with my back to the tree, with arms around my legs
And I could hear the soft crinkle of the crisp leaves, it begs
I felt a tingle as the wind whisked down my pyjama top, contrive
And with that glorious feeling, I was glad to be alive.

Written for Christine.

## 207. JEALOUSY

Why do you have that jealous feeling?
You are in need of emotional healing
I am saddened, oh so deeply
Because I cannot express to others my true feelings, completely
This is making me feel so ill
When all the time it is you who needs to take a pill!

## 208 HALO OF HAWTHORN

From the Hawthorn so sharp
To the playing of the Harp
From the cold ice of day
To the warmth come May
From the Halo of Hawthorn
To feelings, not forlorn
From the sin of misunderstandings
To glad tidings
Glad tidings and good cheer
Ever sincere, for Heaven is here.

## 209. SPECIAL WORDS II

We knew each other for such a long time
Had been married for 35 years
But fine memories I have of him
Remembered through my sorrowful tears
I felt so alone when he passed on
After always being together
But he will always be with me
And I know now that he will be free from pain, altogether
David was so caring and kind
A nicer man you could not find
I will LIVE to be like him every day
And be closer to both him and God in this way, I pray.

Written for Eva.

## 210. MY POEM - SPECIAL WORDS

One day I received a sudden knock
A terrible blow, an awesome shock
I was told of my Sons' death you see
A desperate time ahead for my Husband, and me
He was killed while crossing a railway line
He had not, for his stupor, taken notice of the sign
My Husband was so much in a bad way
That he did not get over it up to the day
When three years later he was taken too
Now on my own, what was I to do?
I'm in residential care at this time
But let me continue with this rhyme
I am well looked after, though my loved ones are gone
But FINE memories linger on
Of my Husband and Son, the BEST of men
AND I am sure they are being looked after too, in Heaven.

Written for Brenda.

## 211. MEMORIES OF MY SON

My Son was taken from me when he was a young man
A mans' man, but a motorbike he ran
But he was not like other Sons
And my memories of him are happy ones
Of climbing trees
In a Summers' breeze
Of breaking Church windows
And scrubbing his toes
Of taking prize leeks
And selling them for keeps
Of working on a farm
In the countryside, calm
Of being a Market Gardener
His very first JOB, with nature
Yes, my memories of him are happy ones
But it's a pity he had to be another "Fonz"
Yes he enjoyed life in full and gave me such pleasure
And still does so, he is my treasure.

Written for Joan.

## 212. JUNES' POEM

When I am feeling low
I sometimes think of my Mother, Mary so
I remember her love and laughter, her being full of carry-on
And of her being a wonderful cook, especially someone to lean
upon
I also wish my Husband Derek could be here every day, too
Because he is the best man ever, not only in my view
But most of all I'd love to be back home
With Derek and my fine memories and to have all my friends
come
To come to visit us there
Because I know that they all care, very much.

## 213. ON VANESSA II

Vanessa, you are the Sister I never had
I want to protect you through all the bad
When you hurt, I hurt too
I am there, whatever you do
I feel what you feel
Pain, fear, anger, all that is real
So if suicidal thoughts come, whichever day
Come to me and we'll make them fade away
Togetherness, of which friends and blessed
My love for you I have confessed.


## 214. YOUR POEM - NORMALITY!

I told him of last night
About one young girls' plight
The girl he'd met only once before
But knowing she was a friend of mine, thought of her he'd see
more
My heart I'd poured into a rhyme
And when he read it had to sit for a time
Because tears built up inside him, was this a crime?
A feeling which had not been felt for quite some time
But a hug and a kiss from me, for this long awaited feeling,
endurance
Was all that was needed for reassurance
This is reality
He's back to normality!

## 215. ASHAMED

I feel so guilty and ashamed
But my heart is too inflamed
I feel as though I have let every-one down
And I am so agitated that I could go to town
I am fed up with this feeling
When will I get my life in order? And in so doing with this
shame, dealing?

Written for Kevin.


## 216. LOGIC

With Mental Illness a certain amount of logic needs to be used
At varying stages, so as not to be confused
We have the ability to talk ourselves around, and out of it
That's better than saying confound it, I don't want to know about
it
If we look at other peoples' problems we will find
That theirs' are worse than ours, not so kind
But it will make us feel a damned sight more confident
AND, a hell of a lot more competent.

Inspired by Trevor.


## 217. SPECIAL WORDS

Dear Mam, words of love I wish to express
I am missing you so very much I must confess
I sincerely hope that you are keeping well
And will come to see me again sometime soon
I love to have conversations with you
And this rhyme is to let you know how much you mean to me,
too.

Written for Sheila.

## 218. THE OTTERS

Bonnie and cute is the otter
In and out of the water, nothing is a matter
Skilfully playing in the pool of a stream
Whilst overhead the sun sends out beam after beam
Out of the water now, shaking off the excess
Pairing up in the Spring, making breeding a success
Soon there will be many more playing happily
And I can watch them joyfully.


## 219. LOVE / HATE

Freud had a theory
A life-long study
But what do I know?
Let me tell it so
Many years ago as a child
The truth having emerged and thus compiled
I loved a person and held him/her in great esteem
Only to be left alone to dwell and tears to team
Over those days and especially nights I wept
And horrid secrets to myself I kept
Eventually turning love into hate
Now, I must that hatred try to abate
In order to put my life back in order
So that hate never leads to bad actions, even murder.

## 220a. SHAUNEE-LEIGH

I'd like to tell you my story
Of how I lost my baby
This wasn't easy to write
So, please listen to my plight
It began when my best friend died in October (1993), yet another funeral
And when I came down for it, it was a bit pointless because in the end I couldn't go
When I faced those Cemetery gates
I just could not go through
My boyfriend and I had fallen out whilst in Scotland
But got back together again down here
I moved into a Hostel for women
But alas there was to be no cheer
We would shop-lift through the day
In order to get money for drugs
And unknown to me I had fallen pregnant
And my boyfriend was now in prison
I was in a Rehab. Centre at this time
And simply thought that I was constipated
Only to find out that I was 16 weeks pregnant and due on August 7th (1994)
I got a house back here at the end of May
But unfortunately next door to a Heroin dealer and the first thing she did
Was to bring around a syringe full of Heroin
So I got hooked once again
And went back into the Rehab Centre, now the middle of June
And I was put onto Methadone, a Heroin substitute
Detoxed to 5mls by the time I went into labour
They stopped my labour pains with Diaphramorphine and I was sent back to the Rehab Centre
That was Wednesday, come Thursday I went for a scan at a different Hospital
They told me that my baby was fine, but small
And that SOME of the fluid was gone
When I went back for another scan the nurse was extremely worried
Because ALL of the fluid was gone!

My waters had broken
Now I was sent to see a Consultant as an emergency
But mine was on holiday and so I saw another
He told me to come for a scan a week later
A nurse told me I could not use buses
and that I had to watch in case I got Knocked
As this would put my baby into stress
Now, by my dates I had 1½ weeks to go
The hospital had my dates wrong going off the size of my baby
But I know I was right because of the time my boyfriend went into
prison
Late that night I started to get really bad pains
But the nurse wouldn't call a Doctor or and Ambulance
Morning staff did because other patients had complained
But when I reached the hospital I was told abruptly that my baby
was dead
I was left alone then, and finally I gave birth to Shaunee-Leigh
at 4 o'clock
Her head had been squashed a bit because her head had been out
for some time
And they had me lying on my side with my legs together (my
Sister noticed)
One of the nurses got kicked out of the room for saying
"You are a soft bitch for crying", when my baby was dead!
Shuanee-Leigh was 3lb 14oz with long curly black hair
Perfect in every way
She was my little girl
And never to be forgotten, ever!!! To be REMEMBERED in this
poem every day.

Written for Leysa.

## 220b. SHAUNEE-LEIGH II - LOVE, MUM

As soon as I got out of Hospital and my boyfriend out of jail
We went to see a Solicitor, because now getting Income Support
meant that I was entitled to apply for "Legal Aid"
I hadn't been able to claim Income Support
And for that same reason, the Hospital had to pay for Shaunee's
funeral
We gave a full statement of everything that "I" could remember
happening
But was turned down for "Legal Aid"
I appealed under the grounds of Mental Distress to myself
And eventually was granted the Legal Aid
Then we had to wait for different reports to come back from
different Specialists
The wait was for over one and a half years
And what I received were pages and pages of words which I did
not understand
But basically it said that one Hospital was denying most of my
existence
And the Rehab Centre was saying that I hadn't complained of
pains
However, one Hospital did not realise that they were being sued
so they passed on my papers
At the moment, they are the only ones I have to go ahead with at
Court
But I understand that once one set is received, the others will have
to be done, too
My Barrister told me that I may lose the case because I was a drug
user "Junkie"
And that if I did, I would probably be offered an out of Court
settlement
I do not want the money!!
All I want is for the Hospitals to admit to their many mistakes
But I was told that the "Legal Aid Board" would make me accept
the money OR, they would stop paying for the case as they would
think money would be better than making a few Hospital
embarrass themselves by admitting liability!!

So, I feel that I cannot win either way!
And Shaunee-Leigh will never rest in peace until the day
When those responsible for her death
Confess of their mistakes with their own breath!
May God bless Shaunee-Leigh through and through
And may all Love her as much as I do.

Written for Leysa.


## 221. T.V.

At the T.V. set we sit and stare
Watching whatever is on there
And of other things we aren't aware
Just as well they don't come as a pair!


## 222. FISH TANK

Rippling water as it breaks
And bubbles on top it makes
Fish aswimming to and fro
Just watch the .......... things go!


## 223. COFFEE TABLE

This is where we put at rest
Our coffee cups, but what a pest
From our armchair we raise ourself
It would be much easier to put up a shelf!

## 224. AT THE BEACH

Off we go to the beach
With bucket and spade, the sands we reach
In and out the waves they come
Washing away my sand castles, I beg "leave me some!"

## 225. WINDOW (DELAVAL WARD)

Prop up the window
Let the wind blow through
Prop it up with a shoe
But mind THAT smell, pooh-ah!

## 226. COMMODE

On the commode
I lighten my load
A better chair I never rode
"Do not enter", I forbode!

## 227. INJECTION

Pinning me down
Not messing around
In goes the needle like a dart
I'll get you back with a rasping fart!

## 228. MEDICATION TIME

Line up in the queue
Stepping forward to
Take our pills, just a few
As we ought'a do
It's Smartie time!


## 229. PEN TO PAPER

I put pen to paper
But what do I write?
Best sooner than later
The whole blooming world needs putting right!


## 230. A DRIPPING TAP

Listen to that tap
Drip, drip, drip
I can't even have a nap
Now I need to pay a trip, trip, trip!


## 231. A BOTTLE OF POP

When we are thirsty
Out comes a bottle of pop
And always when we're in a hurry
We can't get off the top!

## 232. COOKING

All the family come to tea
And I cook to all their wishes
Empty plates are left to see
Now who does all those dishes?!!


## 233. GARDENING

A tidy garden is a thing of beauty
Blooming flowers everywhere
But mowing the lawn is a tiresome duty
And weeding gives me a pain in the back, I swear!


## 234. A BOWL OF FRUIT

On the table stands a bowl of fruit
Apples, oranges, pears and grapes
But when it comes to eating bananas
We'll end up swinging from tree to tree like apes!


## 235. BUSES

A bus, some need to travel around
Especially when it's into town
But to the fellow motorist I say
"Don't they always get in the bleeding way!"

## 236. NEWSPAPERS

Newspapers tell us all the news
From the paper boy we never refuse
Knowing that in the morning we will awake
To nothing that's true, always fake!

## 237. A PAIR OF CURTAINS

Once opened they let in the sunshine
And when too bright they can be partly closed for some time
But when at night the sun goes down
We close them and hide in a dressing gown.

## 238. TEA TOWEL

When we wash the dishes clean
And when no dirty marks can be seen
Then with a tea towel, the dishes we wipe
But then with it, after that, the wasp we swipe!

## 239. BARE WALLS

Walls can be nicely decorated
With pictures and plates hanging there
But when there is nothing up there hung
At those bare walls we blooming well stare!

## 240. RAIN CLOUD

With the wind blows the cloud
Hear the thunder rattling out loud
With that, feel the rain onset
Forgotten umbrellas, now everyone's wet!


## 241. CAR WASH

I hate washing my car
But I must after travelling so far
Because I find it is a terrible sight
Not just with muck, but also birds' ...........!


## 242. LEAFLETS

Splashed with information
Of the right combination
It'll tell you all you want to know
So, to hell with it, just go with the flow!


## 243. PLASTIC BAGS

Always we pick up some polythene
When on shopping we are keen
And when at last we've bought the lot
Peeping THROUGH the holes is what we've got!

## 244. BOOKS

Books we have are a must
On topics which ought to be discussed
And as we PRESS onward
We find that we're no further forward!


## 245. WALLPAPER (SMOKING ROOM)

Pretty wallpaper on the walls
Of dainty flowers and leaf that falls
But in the smoking room we cough
Whilst looking at wallpaper that is hanging off!


## 246. ASHTRAY

Whatever the weather we light up our stuff
Like a chimney smoking we puff
So, whether roasting hot or frozen stiff
See the ashtray, smell that whiff!


## 242. MY BOYS

What a pair of rascals they are
Always playing with a radio controlled racing car
And when the batteries run out
Then they run in and shout
"Mam, can we have some more?!"

## 248. SUNDAY DINNER

I love a Sunday roast
And I always like to boast
That my Mothers' Yorkshire puddings are best
And that way, I get a rest!


## 249. HIS SMELLY SOCKS

His socks they smell a lot
In fact they honestly trot
On wash days, I'd much rather say, "I forgot"
And leave them there to rot!


## 250. WINDOWSILL

A red-tiled windowsill
Usually stays empty 'till
I spot the ledge
And I plonk my backside on the edge!


## 251. BOREDOM

Nothing to do but watch T.V.
And even then it's repeats we see
So instead we suck on a toff -
ee, Can't you tell we're really ............ off!

## 252. WARDROBES

In the wardrobes we hang our clothes
But where the hangers go nobody knows
Only the doors keep swinging open
And I'm sick of closing them, it's that blooming often!


## 253.  A RETRIEVER

A dog so gorgeous never have I seen
And its' coat so golden, with a lovely sheen
But you certainly know when it's been
'Cos there's hairs all over, and now I'm not so keen!


## 254. BINGO

Sitting at the table with dabbers at the ready
On your marks, ready, steady ...
Off we go, numbers marking
Then "Here you are" so shouting!
Bingo!


## 255. SPECTACLES

Without them we are short-sighted
Or we can even be long-sighted
But one thing's for sure
It's the only cure
And is better than being on all fours looking for lenses!

## 256. MY BED

At night in my bed I go
And where my dreams come from I do not know
But one thing I do know is when I wake up
I wish that I'd not had that extra cup!


## 257. MY BED II

Many happy hours I have spent
When into slumber I deeply went
In late afternoon up I sit
Oh, I do so like to stay in my pit!

Inspired by Vanessa.


## 258. LOVE, LIFE AND REALITY

The mind takes over everything
You can't seem to do anything
To take away the thoughts inside
All you want to do is run and hide
To have a drink when you're down
Will only make you sad and frown
The tears begin to run from your eyes
You keep asking why?
Why does this keep happening?
Why can't we seem to do anything?
If only we could see
Love, life and reality.

Written by Vanessa.

## 259. LIFE IS WORTHLESS

Life is worthless
With no care
From either here or there
If only things could be alright
We have to have strength and fight
Without courage there is no future
No future, no life, no meaning at all
Life becomes worthless to us all.

Written by Vanessa.

## 260. LIFE

Clouds gather, as shadows grow
A flash of light, and down below
Fire's rage in brilliant red
Peace ruled supreme, for man is dead.

Anon.

## 261. THE MEANING OF LIFE
## "BILLS' THEORY OF RELATIVITY"

At 48 I'm getting old
Not a child, or so I'm told
Growing up is hard and rough
But after death gets really tough

Standing here on earthly ground
My thinking's getting very profound
Bare your feet and feel the world
Feel in touch, your tootsies curled

Life's confusing, to find a role!
Find you feet, and find you soul
You seek a meaning, ask that tree
Just feel alive, those legs are free

What, why, where, sort that life
Just stay cool, avoid that strife
You ask those rabbits, "Wot's it mean?"
"Eat and sleep man", that's the scene

The stress of life may lead to booze
And so the issue will confuse
Quality of life, you'll often hear
Or simply screw it, have a beer!

Written by W.H.H, 10 June, 1996.

## 262. OTTERBURN TEATIME

Who is Rachel, what is she
She's a word, rhymes with cuddlee
Rounded and Rachel both have R's
Rachel means kindness
As she seriously stares
Kindness itself with pudding and pears.

Written by Rufus.

## 263. THE FIGHT

I feel no-one is my friend
I feel everyone just pretends
Laughing and joking behind my back
I'm never good enough to join their pack

Are these thoughts my own?
Am I not alone?
In thinking everyone's out to get me
And believing everyone's trying to trick me

I cannot sleep at night
It turns into one big fight
Everyone sleeping around me everywhere
The only cub awake in the big lions' lair

When will it vanish?
How can it be banished?
Taking the sadness from out of my life
By slicing and cutting my flesh with a knife

The wave is still here
It will not disappear
Fighting the feelings of hurt and pain
Fighting the need to self-harm again.

Written by Dawn.

## 264. DEPRESSION

Depression is an illness so they say
An illness that will go away
Take your medicines every day
The poison will drive the madness away
Look for a light at the end of the day
But as you awake from a drugged sleep
The light's gone away
You start your treatment over again
Just another start of a depressing day.

Written by Ken.

## 265. I WISH I COULD SEE THEM TONIGHT

When we meet on the level from East to West with brothers just
TRUE and upright
I miss friends and faces of those I loved best and I wish I could
see them tonight
I miss the laughs, the old stories and songs
The smiles and faces of the happy souls left us, whose drifted
along and I wish I could see them tonight
I still feel the old deacons hand who brought me from the
darkness to light
"Tho" rest from his toil in a far better place and I wish I could
see him tonight
How often have I listened to brothers grown old whose voices are
hushed and whose hearts have grown cold
I wish I could see them tonight
The happy hours spent, often the memory returns
But the faces have passed from my sight
Oh I wish I could see them tonight.

Written by Ken.

## 266. FLY FREE

Fly free little bird - fly free
The door of your cage is open
The sky is full and is yours to explore
I wish you soft breezes to glide on
And warm sands to find your rest and peace in -

I'm bound by my feelings to miss your song
You're no longer trapped inside
You're free now go:

Fly high and long
Sing your song loud and clear
Leave nothing for the tomorrow's ahead
Live the now - that is real.

Written by Julie.

## 267. CHEF

I did enjoy your visit -
Have a nice weekend
And we'll enjoy your gateau
May it never end

I expect some company
For a day or two -
Your fame will spread
Far and wide and I will
Need gateau No. 2

When I'm rich and famous
You'll remember me
But my nom de plume is Queenie

When I appear on T.V. -
Send your lovely smile and
Tell them "I know Queenie
Who had a lovely time, in the
Freeman Penthouse
Eating all the food!"

Written by GladyS.

## 268. DELIGHT OF OUR LIVES

We must praise the chefs and handmaidens
Meals are a delight every day
Unsung and unseen you serve food fit for our queen
So its time for attention to pay

Breakfast is super and served with a smile -
Lunch a continual surprise
The curry I like particularly lamb
And lasagne a sight for sore eyes

Restaurant I love (and I'm so short of breath)
but get there each day I will
When this leaflet I found
Put my feet to the ground
For a Gateau like yours beats my pill

If you entered our ward
We would stand up and clap
To show our appreciation
On radio I'll go to let everyone know
the talent you have here on tap.

Written by Gladys.

## 269. CHEF II

Did you get my little note?
Full of praise for you
I do require an answer Chef
So pick up pen and do

You may think 'she's micey
With nothing else to do
It's true!
Not exactly micey but -
On the steroids high

I keep my ward amused like this
So do not take offence
My name is Queenie that's for short
Can you work that out?

## 270. IN THE BEGINNING

Doctor oh doctor my throat is so sore
Ice cream I crave
So I slink out the door
Don't wish to miss you so
I fly down the hall -
Please don't desert me -
Do not at all

No Jill and no doctor and now I've no voice
As I can't talk now I've no choice
But to write down though
It comes out in rhyme!
This book won't last long -
For a hundred or two line
Shortage of paper - its always the same
I'll write on lieu apar and then on wall
Or maybe wall paper then I wouldn't run out
I hope

Later .........

No doctor no Jill
No Ron and no voice
Running out of everything
So I've no choice
But to buy book and pen
Which I try to avoid -
As disaster will follow as
My mind is now void

Poetry leaps out -
Will not let me be
This pen has unleashed
This deep hidden me

The paper attracts and the pen I can't free
My puzzle will suffer can't concentrate now
And foolscap notebook
Will follow this on !

Don't laugh I did try to avoid this
Plague poetry
But
Someone up there is laughing at me

I've bags full of rubbish
Just like this one
Type out a book
And sell for a song?

Mind's ticking over and puzzle is dead
Steroids - I'll blame them
Why blame my head?

Penthouse for me and a wonderful view
10 to 4 now and nobody wants me today
I want to go home I've been here a week
Go on the prowl a doctor to seek
Get my tests done
Do what you like
Friday's the deadline I've got things to do

It's Bank Holiday and there's shopping I know
Want to go out on Saturday night
Cannot dance here it wouldn't be right!
Can't sing, cannot dance, can't talk
And slow when I walk - but my mind's
Working overtime and clear as a bell!
Is it the steroids or just the new book?
It looked so innocent when I picked it up
Or, is it the pen?
I'll throw it away but, the damage is done
And I need it, it's a drug
So, I'm addicted to paper and pen -
Typewriters too, these rhymes have to be booked

So much is happening and
My mind's in a whirl
If the doctor had caught me
There'd be no need for a rhyme
I'd gone for ice cream and
Did not waste the time

So, it's the sore throat to blame
For this poetic plight and if
I don't write it down t'will be
A bloody long night
'Cos it won't go away now and this
Book will get full
You must think I'm a dope
If it comes any faster shorthand I write
As I cannot keep up with this un-miserable blight.

Written by Gladys.

## 271. MY FRIENDS

I am proud to be here with you
It's really quite a treat -
I've told you of my mother
She's a lady hard to beat
I'm very glad to have her but
She isn't here

You all made me so welcome
I really love you all
We'll have to buy a gateau and
Have ourselves a ball

So girls, lets all be getting better
And have a glass or two
But when we are parted
I'll remember you!

Written by Gladys.

## 272. THE STAFF

Chocolate can't say thank you
For your marvellous care -
Poetry says it better with wine
If I dare

QE over at Gateshead
Could learn a tip from you
(I know it's not nice to complain)
But when you're ill in bed
The last thing you are needing
Is verbal tap on the head

No smiles or comfort for daughter Jill
Last year in September -
Operation not much fun and no cheer to remember
NO good morning, how are you - quite beyond belief
So I took Christopher to school and left the work to wait -
Kittens had to stay alone - couldn't leave Jill to this fate

My turn next but just two days
In that prison cell
I won't go there again
It's like a taste of hell!

So raise your glass and wish me well -
You have done me proud.

Thank you

273. QUEENIE

Who's the mysterious Queenie?
Queenie pussy-cat
Kaseem knows and Christopher
But they will not reveal my name
Or no pocket-money will be issued
What a crying shame
Bribery - yes, so what!

Written by Gladys.

## 274. LAST DAY

Up in the morning
Breakfast in bed -
Shower and hairdo
And doctor to led (poet's licence)
ECG first and doc takes a look
And asks have I finished my new little book?

Yes, I'll say proudly and I've orders galore
Give me your £2 and add to my store
Of cash for your cause -
I'll help it a treat
And get this thermometer set on its' feet.

Written by Gladys.

## 275. DAVID

A man in my ward is making donation
T.V. set I think will be had
Give me autograph sir and in this book
You can be Sir Galahad.

Written by Gladys, 30 May, 1996.

## 276. THE ICE MAN
## (DEDICATED TO TONY)

The Ice Man knew some stuff
He never had his mind set on agro
Because the Ice Man was so cool
He never broke any rules
And because the Ice Man loved himself
And he was never left on the shelf
Like a tin of corned beef
He never cleaned his teeth
And then the poor man got cramp
And became a star on "Rising damp".

Written by J.C.B.

## 277. THE LOVER

The lover came down
The lover lost his crown
But lover of Heaven came to the town
The men and the ladies came close to a fight
But they were afraid of the night
So let's give a cheer
Go to Whitley Bay and let our hair down
Rocking away in the town
And never let me down
But let's have and ice-cream
And all fall down laughing in the crowds.

Written by J.C.B.

## 278. THE CHOCOLATE KID

The Chocolate Kid
Couldn't bid
Unless it was with Sid and Nancy
Looking Kind'a fancy
So Chocolate Kid
Make that bid
Never fear
Because I am here
So go to bed
Sleepy head
And come with me on a trip to the skies
And I'll wave to you good-bye
And say cheerio
And say it with love.

Written by J.C.B.


## 279. FLY IN THE DANDRUFF

The fly in the dandruff
Went in a huff
The fly never liked soup
But the fly just knew it was really cheap
So he got brewers' droop
And he never really got a look
Because it was soup
But could it be his soup
Or a fly in the dandruff.

Written by J.C.B.

## 280. THE CROW

The crow under the snow
Never went home
The snow was too deep
But we never heard a peep
As they said let's reap
The crow never heard a peep
Until he came and swept the floor
And there were noises
Goodness knows
It's those crows
Making a cake with a recipe book from "Bearo"
So let's give a cheer
And say hip hip hooray
Happy holiday!

Written by J.C.B.

## 281. CUSTODY

Summer is here
But Autumn draws near
Flowers in abundance grow
But colder winds are about to blow
With each golden leaf that will fall
Comes Natures' call
And animals will hide
No longer with young at their side
Each bird has flown
Each one, the parent's outgrown
Bare trees will be left to view
The weather has changed, that is true
A carpet of gold to be trodden upon
Remembering when I gave birth to my first son
Memories rendered one by one
Because MY YOUNG will stay with me when the battle is won.

## 282. CONTENTMENT

Why am I not content?
Content with what I've got
I am steadily going into debt
Because I want the bloody lot!
A better house
A better car
A better holiday
Under a different star
Better than you've got
Better by far
When will this craze end?
So a better life I can spend!

Inspired by Roy.


## 283. ISOLATION

I am old
A story I could have told
But now I am alone
With my memories, not even a telephone
All my friends and relatives have passed on
I now have no-one to rely upon
When I die I may not, for some time, be found
I won't be heard because I won't make a sound
Where is our caring society?
Please take note of this reality!

Inspired by Roy.

## 284. SPEND TIME WITH ME

I am a child
But was I wanted?
I am left to be wild
How can this be prevented?
You leave me each day, and work you attend
All I ask is that time with me you spend
At night, you socialise
When will you wake up and realise?
You leave me with money in my pocket
But the only love I feel is in a heart-shaped locket
The latter because you are never there
Do you really care?

Inspired by Roy.

## 285. SCREWED UP

Because of my upbringing I am in a bad way
Drugs and drink were for me every day
From being young I knew nothing else, and now
My organs are damaged, but somehow
I must try to gain strength to resist
Instead of constantly getting high and p****d!

Written for Leysa.

## 286. ANOREXIA

Once I was 4 ½ stone
So thin that my face was drawn in
My boyfriend had to almost carry me around
And one day my sister walked right passed me, because I was so
much like a pin!

Written for Leysa.




## 287. TERRIBLE THEFT

I had everything ready for my babies birth
But alas she died before she was born
And when they heard that my baby had died
They stole everything from my house, my fate sworn
No-one gave me help because I was on my own
And on a cold bare floor of stone
I had to lay down for the night
A vivid memory, a pitiful sight.

Written for Leysa.

## 288. MIND

My thoughts are confused
Hard to find my way
My brain is being used
By what I cannot say
My mind is not my own
Flows to a different beat
My power I find has grown
But is not yet complete
Time will find the answer
To problems I know inside
A metaphysical cancer
I feel my brain has died.

Written by Adam

## 289. LIFE II

The mighty warlords are on the wing
The end of mankind, is the song they sing
The world and its' wonders, he would wreck
All for a lousy, monthly pay cheque.

Written by Rufus.

## 290. MY POEM - TREVOR

Let me tell you of my troubled life
Full of both pain and strife
When I was twelve years old my father died
Which meant that my mother had to work to feed the family
My elder brother used to force me to go to bed while he
entertained girls
And he would give me beating after beating
I still have flashbacks to this day
And to my dwelling on the past, is added yet more problems
I have four children of my own, the eldest being ten, the youngest
three
But alas I cannot get to see them as much as I'd like to
Each time I do see them I am overjoyed
But then when I leave them I am absolutely gutted
However I know that they love me, because I am still their Dad
And as they grow older they will want to see more of me, too
I may keep in touch with my eldest by letter
Something which, until now, had not entered my mind
But most of all I must pray for God to take away bad thoughts of
self-harm
As I must LIVE to see the day when my children come to me
Now, I am calm.

## 291. DEAR DAD

Dear dad, I feel lost without you
So much so that it sometimes effects what I do
You are always on my mind
Why did I have to lose someone so good and kind?
Not only were you lost
But at what cost
Why did you have to suffer so?
With cancer of the bowel, was this the way you had to go?
I could not bear to see you suffer in this way
And I could not cry on your funeral day
I was so cut up about what had happened
And still have not cried, not because I know I shouldn't
At the time you found out you were dying
I found out that I was pregnant, but could only see you crying
My daughter you never knew
Because six months later you were taken from view
But Dad, I remember some of the good times, too
Like going for walks as the warm breeze blew
I hope that as time goes by I will remember more of this
And live my life knowing that you are in good hands, now, and
sign off with a kiss.

Written for Linda.

## 292. THE YOUNG DRAGON

I am the young dragon in this story
For now, my flame burns quite low
I need to learn how to behave in society
To my parents I look to be taught, so
I am a young dragon
My mother has left my father for his best mate
She entertains and socialises, drinking all of the time
So, I get beating after beating from him, that was my fate
The young dragon sees nothing else
Waiting outside Pubs and scared to go home
So what did I do? I started drinking from her bottle, replacing
with water
Hoping that I could forget or that the belt buckle would not feel
like stone
The young dragon is easily led
And starts to use drugs like other dragons do
The cravings were there now
The drugs I was addicted to
The young dragon learned to steal
With the money drugs would be bought
Now with boyfriend, both hooked
To enter a rehab centre, help sought
The young dragon found out she was pregnant
Whilst her boyfriend was in jail
But the baby gave her hope
Hope to begin a new life, no more needles or smoke to inhale
The young dragon went into hospital
Where she was snubbed for being a "Junkie"
And because more bad dragons were there
Due to neglect she lost her baby
The young dragon has felt stigma at its' worst
The young dragon has felt the harshness of their flames
But the young dragon is tougher than most and holds back
And in the young dragon now burns an INNER flame.

Written for Leysa.

118

## 293. THE YOUNG DRAGON II

Long is the story of the young dragon, not to blame
Who felt stigma at its' worst
Now in the young dragon burns an inner flame.
Raging to be out, to burst
Into a huge fire from the depths of within
To extinguish, endeavour
For the young dragon must be free of memories and sin
To purify, for ever!


## 294. THREESOME (NIGHT-SHIFT)

Who's on duty?
Oh no!
Zany Janie and Sheryle the peril
But wait a minute
Oh yes!
We crave for Dave!!
But a team of three
Who are fancy free
You'll do for me!

## 295. NORTHUMBRIA

Northumbria of peels and fells
Of the bothy where the shepherd dwells
of Cragside where lived Lord Armstrong
Far from the cities bustling throng
Hexham Abbey and Finchale Priory
Of Bamburgh close to the grey North Sea
Of the Cheviot country and Wooler
And the Northumbrian burr
Of Alnwick Castle and the Dukes' meadows
Thro' which the Aln flows
The river North Tyne and Belsay
Chollerford Camp when Roman soldiers held sway
Northumbria land of bog and heather
Of gill, hillside, fog and misty weather.

Written by Duncan Gray, 10 April, 1996.

## 296. CUMULOUS CLOUDS

White sailed galleons sailing across a tropic ocean
A white tower when a knight-errant looks for his love
A long-necked, white maned Arab steed
The lost legion led by a Roman eagle
Distant white-peaked Himalayan mountains
A woman in a modern dance routine
These moving clouds fill my imagination with many images.

Written by Duncan Gray, 10 April, 1996.

## 297. THE SMUGGLERS

The Frenchie schooner is anchored in the bay
Its' Captain, Michael De La Fay
On the beach await the Kentish smugglers
With their pack horses getting rather restless
A cloud crosses the moon and three boats
Laden with barrels of brandy and wines
Make for the beach of Cloven Cove
Silks from the low countries too
Laced petticoats from Bruges
For m' Lady Caroline Rouge
Four star brandy for the sessions Justice of the Peace
Whose name is Sir Joshua Samuel Reece
Wines for the table of Lord Hastings
Wines from Burgundy and Bordeaux
Silks to make into evening dresses
For Lady Fanshore and the Hon. Mrs Nora Lascelles
The three boats return to the schooner
And the schooner, up-anchor and out of the bay
The smugglers are led by O'Shae
Along the rough and rugged smugglers way.

Written by Duncan Gray, Late March, 1996.

## 298. ON LYNN

She paints, she talks in a quiet way
She is as fresh as the flowers in May
She reminds me of some placid stream
Where-in silver fishes gleam
A picture which she painted for me
Was of foal and Exmoor pony.

Written by Duncan Gray

## 299. SUNRISE

Another day is born as the sun rises in glory over the rim of the
earth
A golden radiance fills the valley and turns the lake into a sheet
of molten gold
Darkness has gone in the Eastern sky
I think on Icarus whose wings were made of wax
He, of Greek Mythology, who plunged to Earth
As the rising sun melted the wing when the sun is a blood-red
ball
Rising up above my horizon
I have also seen opaque colours in the dawn
Then a blending together by the eternal artist.

Written by Duncan Gray, March, 1996.

## 300. SUNSET

Senacharib with his chariots of fire
Roared across the sky at eventyr
The very streams ran with blood
The Western sky was a scarlet flood
Until Senacharib faded away
Unto the end of common day
In the twilight that surrounded me
Hid amongst the trees elf and pixie.

Written by Duncan Gray, 16 March, 1996.

## 301. OF SHIPS, SEAMEN AND THE SEA

The sea, the sea, the deep, dark sea
Full of moods, of mystery
The Arab dowh in the Gulf of Akaba
Piloted by Abu Ben Ali with a star
The Roman galley, oars flashing in the sun
Of a sunny day in the Mediterranean
The Norse long ship ploughing thro' Northern waves
Vikings were a free race, never slaves
The high-pooped galleon "Santa Sobela"
Spanish seamen journeyed to lands afar
"H.M.S. Victory" at Cape Trafalgar
A diabolic machine of war
The clipper ship "Cutty Sark" - Queen of the seas
Carrying rum and spices from the Indies
Paddle - Steamer "Burma Star" on the Irawadi
In its' engineering nothing shady
The Lucitania, P & O's luxury ocean liner
'twixt London and New York, Captain Steiner
Of new maritime innovations - what a range
From reed raft to Hydrofoil - what a change
The ancient Severn Coralle
To the modern ferry
The seamen who fall for the sea
Deep and full of mystery
Man, except the Dutch, has never tamed the sea
The Dutch have faced the North Sea bravely
Their dykes have held quite secure
Long may Dutch engineers endure
The sea, the wildly untameable sea
Seething, foaming, treacherous sea.

Written by Duncan Gray, March, 1996.

## 302. ELSDON

Shy Elsdon, what glories are thine
And breezes from the moorland blows in like wine
Thy moot-hills reclining and dreaming of yore
Thy old towered rectory, part of Border war
Thy ancient peel tower that hurled insult against Border-reiver
The Armstrongs, the Elliots, the Milburns, the Fawcets, the Scotts
Jack Armstrong the moss-trooper
They found him on the Otter-caps
Dead from a pistol shot to the head
On the day he should have been wed
Goodbye, then, Elsdon, goodbye
As cumulous sail across a cobalt sky
For all the world like a Norweigan sailing barque
Sailing onward for its Scandinavian harbour
Far from the city "rat race"
On Elsdon common close at hand
Elsdon I bid thee a fond "farewell"
Astride my Claude Butler touring bicycle.

Written by Duncan Gray
Summer, 1942 - aged 15
Amended March, 1996.

## 303. THE LARK

I watched him low-hovering in the Eastern sky
A tiny, feathery messenger of joy
Scattering his glad tidings to the earth below
And as I watched he rose to higher altitudes
'Till but a darkened speck he disappeared from sight
Behind a fleecy rosy-tinted cloud
I waited for my entertainer to descend
And as I waited saw the colours blend
Pale purple, yellow, orange, flaming red
With beating heart I saw my lark appear
Descending in vertical descent
Slow how slow
Seeking with care amongst the waving grasses
And turning watched the Western radiance ebb and die.

Written by Duncan Gray, aged 14.

## 304. GREEN WAS MY VALLEY

Green was my valley, bright at dawn
Green were the trees, the meadow fair
Yet man has come, his schemes have shorn my valley's graces
Oh how grim, how black the ground
Where once waved fields of glittering corn
As I look back o'er fading years I see again the care-free lad
Who used to climb the knarled oak
That championed all in Cotters Wood
And then industry spread her cloak
And snarled: this countryside is mine
Soon shall throb with my pulsating blood
How well industry kept her oath
For where she breathed deep squalor sprang
And countless people clawed for power
They clawed for 'more' for 'more' for 'MORE'
'Till soon the erstwhile, happy core
Was rent from out the countryside
Long have I dreamt of a blushing dawn
To sweep this sacrilege aside
And bring relief to land outworn
Alas! my fading eyes will never see
The day industrie's wheels are stilled.

Written by Duncan Gray, 1943, Aged 16.

## 305. THE HEWER

Black hairy arms and heaving chest
Crouched low in dripping quarters cramped
His grimy singlet exertion damped
Old Dick the miner plied his trade
Whilst listening to the rumbling tubs
Come down the half-mile grade
His aching limbs he never set one moment to ease
But like some panting sweating mole
He burdened deep into the coal
The coal that gives off white heat
And drives the ships which sail the seas
Without old Dick and his marra' Jack
There would be less coal brought up to bank
Less electricity, less guns less tanks
So let us give out heart-felt thanks
And when we finally reach our 'goal'
Remembered must they be.

Written by Duncan Gray, 1940, Aged 13.

## 306. MID SUMMERS' SOLIQUE

A Summer garden full of Hollyhock
And a metal sundial by Joseph Brock
Roses, Lupins and Sunflowers
To pass away the happy hours

One does not need 'A Brain Scan'
When one can enjoy Richard Clayderman
Playing 'English Country Garden'
Or listen to Richard Taubet's 'Old Chelsea'

Geraniums in a window-box display
Are the pride and joy of little Mrs McBrae
She lost her Bob several years ago
Who grew Carnations for a local show.

Written by Duncan Gray, April, 1996.


## 307. SONG OF AUTUMN

Hips and haws and golden leaves
Late swallows departing from the eaves
Yellow stubble in the field
Upturned by the plough of farmer Shield

Chrysanthemums, bronze, rust and white
Autumns pallet rich and bright
I love Autumn, mellow Season
Which Dame nature plans in reason

If I had been an Artist in oils
I should have painted the colours of the soils
The trees, the flowers. the Autumn skies
Many an old countryman's eyes
'See' and so ane nature wise.

Written by Duncan Gray, September 8, 1993.

## 308. LADY DE WINTER

She walked thro' the spindly wood
In a flowing cloak of black
And her breath was as cold as the Matterhorn
Whilst her eyes were icy-green as Alpen glacier
And so she came and so she passed me by
The birds, too, were as silent as I
As I stood in a perpendicular wave of interlacing Beech branches
I heard the pad pad of animal feet
And saw the tiny impressions on the snow

It was December, Christmas approached
How I loved to hear carols sung by Aled Jones
And to watch happiness in children's faces
As the Shell family stand around their Xmas tree
A Barbie doll for little Sue
A Lego set for brother Ian
Cote for Mrs. Shell from Bob her Hubby
An Apple computer for Bob from Helen his wife
A new Rosewood pipe for Grandad Shell
And so Xmas comes and goes
Lovely is the Xmas Rose
Lady De Winter is gone at last
When Snowdrops are of the past.

Written by Duncan Gray, May, 1996.

## 309. THE FOX

The full moon glistened, on your frost laden hide
Winter fur sparkled, as you lay on your side
You looked so peaceful, just having a rest
Just living life, not being a pest

I thought you were fooling, lie low and play dead
I kept my fingers away from your head
I'm trying to help you, bite if you dare
But I saw in your eyes , a vacant stare

Fields full of fun, each side of the road
Didn't you learn the highway code
Full moons' light, from so far away
Called you back from a life full of play

No roads to cross now, rest where you are
It didn't seem right, to move you too far
The following night, you were still there
Stiff and cold, in the moonlights' glare

I stopped again, on my way for a beer
Felt it was time, to move you from here
Picked you up, your eyes open wide
And laid you to rest, down the bankside.

Written by Rufus, December 28, 1993.

## 310. E.C.T.

Eat no breakfast, that's the game
I can manage, just the same
But no tea, at morning time
Is a cruel and wicked crime

The tea withdrawals, they get bad
A caffeine addict, how very sad
Give up beer, no big deal
A different league, no tea, NOT REAL

They owe a lot to Faraday
And other stars to show the way
Electro therapy's lifted my mood
On the grim, grey past, no longer brood

My needle phobia is no more
At three or four, it became a bore
My muddled thoughts no longer mix
At five or six, I enjoyed the fix

Volts over Amps, and resistance in Ohms
Those electrical freeways, the electron roams
Newton and Kirchoff had something to say
Men of vision, they led the way.

Written by Rufus, July 15, 1996.

## 311. E.C.T.(The Way It Used To Be)

A room full of beds is all I saw
As I walked in gown and slippers across the floor
Above each bed a picture hung upon the wall, so plainly painted
And WEIRD calming music from "One flew over the Cuckoos'
Nest", not appreciated.

We were on a "Conveyor belt" of sort
One wheeled out of the other side, from this side another brought
After our treatment we were woken up
With, in our hands, a tea cup.

## 312. LOVE IN SPRINGTIME

What ho, Sir John said she to he
Under the flowing Greenwood tree

Thou art a pretty maid, he said
Fain would I take thy maiden head

Then come, Sir John, said Florentine
And I will give thee love like wine

And we shall have a family
Who'll play beneath the Greenwood tree.

Written by Duncan Gray.

132

## 313. TO AN ENGLISH FRIEND OF LATVIAN ORIGIN ARUIDS OR 'AURO'

There is freedom in the Baltic air today
Celebrations and flowers and display
Latvians raise their eyes when the Latvian flag floats high
Freedom to vote in a National Parliament
After over fifty years of subdued discontent
Freedom to openly worship Christ: read
A free, not a clandestine, press
To speak ones' mind and not to be placed under harrowing duress
The Secret Police have gone: few lament their going
Now that the wind of freedom, like a lusty babe, is blowing.

Unlike some fictional ruritania
Hail Latvia, Estonia and Lithuania
This Christmas will be a happy one for the Baltic peoples
As bells peal forth from high steeples
Across the Baltic lands joyous sounds will ring
As Latvians acknowledge Christ their King
Karl Marx and Lenin, Stalin and Breshnev are shadows now
Young Latvians will forget them as they sturdily grow
They will forget those years of tyranny and remember only what
it is like to be free
The Winter of Discontent is o'er - it's happening as Latvia
prepareth for a gentler Spring.

God Bless Latvia, queen of the Baltic Sea
The peoples' of the free world, solute thee.

Written by Duncan Gray, 1991.

## 314. SMOKE - INHALATION

Human chimneys in the Ardgowan Sitting room
Coughing over and over again
The danger signs are there
Smoking, smoking, smoking
Coughing, women as well as men
A smoking habit that could shorten life
I am a non-smoking individual yet I have inhaled a large amount
of smoke
A bad habit smoking cigarettes, pipe, snuff
And yet a varied number of people smoke, from Oxford dons to
Labourers and Chartered Accountants, from housewives to
female nurses.

Written by Duncan Gray.


## 315. SONG OF AUTUMN

St. Saviours' is decorated with corn sheaves
Autumn fruits and leaves
Christians sing their Hymns of Thanksgiving
In high roofed nave voices reverberating

'Come you joyful people come
Swell the sound of Harvest home
All is safely gathered in
Ere the Winter storms begin'

Hips and haws and golden leaves
Late swallows departing from the eaves
Yellow stubble in the field
Upturned by the plough of farmer Shield

Chrysanthemums: bronze, yellow, rust and white
Autumns' pallet rich and bright
I love Autumn, mellow season
When Dame Nature plans in reason.

Written by Duncan Gray.

## 316. SPRING SERENADE

Springtime is the Season for followers
To pass away those gentle hours
Daffodils, roses, narcissi, tulips, violets
Leave no room for sad regrets
Woodlarks are singing 'mongst the trees
soon primroses will cover leaves
Apple blossom on orchard bough
Skylarks rising heavenward now
Easter time for the religious faith
In Christ's resurrection after death
Happy, happy, happy Springtime buds are opening in the lime

Catkins dance upon the Willow
Daffy down, daffy down dillow
In the Church a Springtime marriage
Complete with grey docile men and carriage
Hare's dance, likewise courting cranes
Misanthropist forget the staines
For lo, above us is a light blue sky
And white clouds, like galleons sailing by.

Written by Duncan Gray.

## 317. WINTER

Winter cold and drear
There is ice upon the mere
Pale shafts of sunlight on the lake
At daybreak

O hag of Winter
Go at last
Become naught but
The past
Let the Spring
Maiden walk o'er
The Lea
Bedecked with ribbons gaily

I shall always remember
The bitter cold of mid December
The icicles upon the bough
In Winter now

O to see the Springtime again
Of mild sunlight after rain
Of wild and golden daffodils
Dancing atop rounded hills
Streams are running bright and cool
Young deer drink from green forest pool
The whole world is awakening to the rustlings of the Spring.

Written by Duncan Gray, March 23, 1994.

## 318. LITTLE BECKY

Little Becky, short for Rebecca was in the Department Store that night, when she disappeared. Her mother was frantic, family and friends searched everywhere.

Unknown to them a lonely ghost had taken a liking to little Becky and had zipped her away to his hiding place in the roof of the building.

Becky was scared, even though she could not see the ghost she was still very afraid. She pleaded for him to let her go. He said that he would let her see her family one more time then she had to be his to keep. Becky agreed.

So, the ghost made her invisible and whisked her off her feet and rushed her downstairs where he put her down to see her mother. Becky could not speak, even though she tried.

"That's enough", he said "You are only upsetting yourself". He whisked Becky up off her feet again in order to carry her off upstairs, when the string of pearls around her neck caught on something and pearls began to drop to the floor slowly, one by one.

Her mother noticed them. The ghost was angry and rushed Becky to the escalator. Her family and friends rushed afterwards following the line of pearls right up into the roof of the building.

Now the ghost was really mad. He showed himself. To everyone's surprise he was nice and seemed gentle. All he wanted was a friend. Becky chirped up "I'll still be your friend!" "I'll come and visit you all the time". The ghost smiled, "Would you still do that?" he asked "Of course", she said, "Love is to share, isn't it?"

Little Becky visited the ghost regularly and so love was shared, wasn't it?

## 319. LITTLE JANE

Little Jane was asked when a child what she would want to be when she was older. Little Jane replied "A Nun".

But in older years it came to her that the meaning of life was not to give up life for one single task or good deeds.

But instead to enjoy life as God INTENDED whilst doing good deeds or tasks on Life's way (journey).

## 320. NORTHUMBERLAND R.I.P.

This Summer, none was brighter
The hills were all of a thrill
Salmon were leapin' the river
Red Deer up on the hill

We sat in some mighty mouthed hollow
Full of hush, plumb to the brim
Saw the big red sun wallow
In crimson and gold and grow dim

We sat there 'till the big mighty moon was gleamin'
And the stars they came out neck and crop
We thought we must surely be dreamin'
With the peace of the world on top

It's the big broad land up yonder
The land where silence has lease
Strange slanting shadows to ponder
Northumberland our county of everlasting peace.

Written by Joe.

## 321. FLY HIGH IN THE SKY
## PUT YOUR DREAMS ON THE PILLOW

Jack and the Beanstalk came to play
Peter Pan is here to stay
His name is Bill, or Rob, or Joe
I don't know which I'm just a Limmito (lick my toe)

When you wake up in the morning
And Confucius say
One if the staff is little Neilie
And Tinkerbell is flying nearly

Barbie the doll that's really Brenda
Then big Sas comes in as tall as he can be
There's a bad lion in the office
Telling tales on me

So now the one that's flying high with Peter Pan
Thinks she can just fly away
But I need her as a mother
And I wish that she would stay.

Dedicated to the one I love.
Narissa.

## 322. ON A JOURNEY

Where beggars wheedled, hitching hikers come
And itching palm hands on to hitching thumb
Small differences in the mendicants - each begs
Benevolence to spare his alms, or legs
And charity dispenses equal gifts
Raising the lowly up, on giving lifts.

Written by Francois Charles.

## 323. FRENCH LIMERICK

Il etait un gendarme a Nanteille
Qui n'avait qu'une dent et qu'un oeiul
Mais cet oeiul solitaire
Etait pleine de mysterie
Cette dent d'importance et d'oiguile.

Written by Francois Charles.

## 324. TERMINALLY ILL

Today I was given news that was bad
I was sickened and my heart felt sad
The reason for my weakness is now clear
Death looms up ahead and I have a fear
Eventually in a chair I will be wheeled
My fate now has definitely been sealed
I must come to terms with what must be
Pray for the end so I will be of pain free
Each day I will live for the next
With other people I will try not to be vexed
Because they may live a longer life than me
And because many more things they will do and see
So I will enjoy what I have got now
And when the time comes before God I will bow
All my fear will be gone on that wonderful day
And all long gone friends and family in Heaven will lead the
way.

## 325. DIVORCE

The time has come to split
You have done a moonlight flit
What am I to do?
Hit the booze, what's a few?
The kids are gone as well
You will poison their minds, I can tell
So, I'll either drown my sorrows, or take an overdose
Or maybe both to bring death close
But all the while
I wish to see your smile
My heart is breaking
Indeed it is aching
For your love once again
Oh dear it's beginning to rain
God's tears of sadness
Once more I long for gladness
Will it head my way
Shall I be happy one day
Right now I feel like crying
And the wrong way out I see, is by dying.

## 326. POST TRAUMATIC STRESS

In court, the things which I have heard said
Just doesn't simply go over my head
I cannot sleep at all right now it seems
Because I remember in my dreams

In a disaster, what I have been put through
Goes through my mind and I feel blue
I cannot stop thinking back
And everything now appears to be black

At work, the things which I have experienced
When death has struck, life no longer prolonged
I cannot rid my mind of memories
And nightmares are envisaged

For to get over death of this sort
More counselling should be taught
Post traumatic stress is day to day - reality
Counselling and support should be the normality.


## 327. FRIDAY 13TH

To me the number 13 means doom
But Friday the 13th is doom and gloom
Having the fear of this number is tolerable, just
But on that fateful day hide I must.


## 328. COUNTING

Constantly counting in my head
Even when I'm in my bed
Everything and anything I count, wherever I tread
Numbers clicking up, like of sheep, but none are said.


## 329. WATER

Everywhere I went I had a glass of water
And if my glass was empty, I felt to fill it I aught'a
People offered me more glasses and jugs of it too
And in the end, I became fed up with water, like you do.

## 330. CLEANING

My home is spotless
Because I am obsessed with cleanliness
Out comes the vacuum and duster
I cannot sit down because I'm always in a fluster
Into my cupboards I dive
Wiping them clean, I never skive
If I don't slow down soon, I will have a nervous breakdown
But first, one more time, in the house let's go to town.


## 331. OUT OF THE DARKNESS

Reach out your hand, my friend
And feel the grip of mine
Take it, and let your melancholy drop from you
Remember, Spring comes re-born with Aprils' dew
Even our darkest doubts quelling
Striking the heart to pulse anew
As life in you renew
Remember, the darkness does not belong to you.

Written by Francois Charles.

## 332. THE DAWN

Hail dawn, when Poebus gins arise
And paints his lovely colours in the morning skies
I who have never painted the birthplace of a Saint
Have seen those colours the eternal brush doth paint
Soft peach and delicate pink and egg-shell blue
Such hanging opaque loveliness that must pass
Like maidens footprints on the dewy grass
Into the mundane happenings of common day
Common I say! And yet the lark still sang
And oer the misty vale his paeons rang
Whilst blue grey shadows lifted from the hills
And I saw a myriad silver rills.

Dedicated to Mrs Lynn Harle
By Duncan Gray.

## 333. WINTER PICTURES

The lofty tracery of elm branches
Looking for all the world as cathedral nave
Shining ice on the dark mere
The silence of the deep woods
Silent save for crackling twigs and tiny padding feet
Crocus' make a splash of colour
Around the base of the bowl of trees
And so Winter goes out and Spring comes in
Soon so soon daffodils will open their faces to pale sunlight.

Written by Duncan Gray.

## 334. NIGHTMARES

I wake up with a fright
Each and every single night
Bad dreams I have while asleep
Creatures and demons at me leap
I am always being attacked
Leaving me in the morning, feeling whacked
Whether bitten by a bat or chased by a man
Try to think a better thought if you can
No more starts of cold sweats for me tonight
Bad dreams are out of mind, out of sight.

## 335. COLD

I am cold
Shivering, so cold
No-one to hold
My arms, enfold
Might I be so bold
The world be told
My life, my soul has been sold
And my flesh will mould
I am old
So very cold
Shivering, cold.

## 336. HAILSTONES

Hailstones at the window
I'd better stay in
The wind is strong, hear the strength of its' blow
I wish I didn't have to listen to the din
It's nice and warm here though
But in my local pub it's warm too, as you know
I enjoy the friendship and company
But while I am sat here I can still see
The scene so fresh in my mind from the other night
The warmth and the comfort, a wonderful feeling, a beautiful
sight.


## 337. MY LEGS & MY LUNGS

My legs are aching and stiff
It's like they are not mine
Not like the legs I once knew
The ones that felt so fine
I used to run and jump, my memories of it are great
But it would be hard for you to imagine, looking at me in this
state
Out of breath so quickly too
My lungs affected by years of smoking, now I cannot have even a
few
If I were a tree, me they would fell
If I were a car, I would be exchanged for a new model
I'll just have to take each day as it comes
Last out this Winter and look forward to Summer suns
One of these days these legs and lungs WILL rest
But first in friendships I will invest
Having family and friends makes a difference
That keeps me going, gives me that extra confidence
Each day I try to keep happy as best as I can
Being careful not to knock over the bed pan
Old age is definitely a burden
But at least I'm not under the knife of a surgeon!

## 338. EYESIGHT & HEARING

My eyesight is fading fast
I long to see properly again, at last
I only see shadows now, blast!
Everything seems to be overcast.

My hearing is impaired
To wear a hearing aid, I never dared
People don't speak loud enough, as if they never cared
Forever left out of it, they don't know how I've fared.


## 339. INCONTINENCE

Do you know what it's like to be embarrassed pray tell?
To feel uncomfortable, and the smell
To have to be bathed by someone else each time
In silence, no laughs, no jokes, it feels like a crime
Why don't my parts work anymore?
Why do I constantly leave puddles on the floor
I hate wearing pads, all of the time like this
But if I don't, I feel vulnerable, they're a miss
It's a pity my brain is still in good working order
Then it wouldn't have been such a torment, or hurt inside like
murder.

## 340. WINTER THOUGHTS

White stippled branches
The snow as pure as a virgin
And yet snow can be sullied
On the Pennines and on the Cheviots the snow lies deep
Towards the coast there is but slush
Those grey days of the Old Hag
Winter can be a dowdy witch
And yet, when the pale sun shines
It lifts human moods.

Written by Duncan Gray.

## 341. XMAS WISHES

With this card comes Christmas cheer
And wishing you well this coming year
Carols sound sweet when children sing
But the words read better, having depth and meaning
The story of Christmas is a lovely one
And quite rightly has been written in song
But children's school plays act it out too
Leaving a wonderful feeling, like after playing a great shot with
a snooker cue
A friendship, a true one is hard to find
Too many people these days are selfish and unkind
Keep up with the darts as well, a game which keeps you amused
And keep your cool, when I beat you next time because -
I've practised.

## 342. LEES' POEM

Whether alone or in a crowd when I sit in a chair
I have the feeling that I will be stuck there
The feeling of weakness both in mind and body comes over me
Somehow I must gain the strength to get free
When I stand up eventually
Let this time be the last, finally.


## 343. MY LOVE FOR YOU, DECLARED

I love you with all of my heart
So much so, that I never want us to be apart
This love I feel has grown more, each day
And I wish to know you better in every way
Think of flowers, scented, so fragrant
Sent with showers of kisses, a love so radiant
Let our love heal us, and finally
Let us bond together, naturally, and eternally
You have given me a meaning in life
A hope, a wish of joy overwhelms me
You are tenderness, and I long for your touch
And I wish to declare my love for you, for all to see.


## 344. LOVE I

I love you so very, very much
But alas I cannot get in touch
To tell you what I have seen
And to ask how you have been
God loves you too, the demons will go
Peacefully sleep, I wish I was there so
I could watch over you and understand how you feel
Love can do many things, but especially heal.

## 345. LOVE II

With each hug you give
For more I crave
Rescue me show me how to live
Don't let me take long ago memories to my grave
I think and dream of you all the time
Make these thoughts reality with this rhyme
Be close to me always
And let loves' passion be ablaze.

## 346. LOVE III

You know, I'm feeling sad
Fighting thoughts that are bad
Oh, what a lad
You would make a wonderful dad
Not just to mine, but perhaps even your own
Loves' seed can be sown
I would like, with you, to do something special
For us both to get leave the same day would be essential
Not your place, not mine
But somewhere that would suit us just fine
To be alone, together
And get to know each other better.

## 347. LEE II

Lee, what a mover
When playing his favourite game of snooker
But he also enjoys the game of darts
And they say "Cor, what fancy sharts!"

## 348. IN LOVE

My head is all in a spin
Everyone is speaking but there's only a din
Because my concentration is far away
In dreamland, where I want to stay

At night lying in bed tucked up tight
Then I reach out to switch off the light
Lying there naked and bare
But alas you are not there

Where are you tonight?
Are you tucked up tight?
I only spoke to you on the telephone
Not for long, and then you were gone.


## 349. BAD THOUGHTS

I was sad because I had not seen my children in over a week
So much so that death I set out to seek
I broke a compact mirror into pieces, small
And I planned to swallow them bit by bit, all
But what stopped me from doing this
Was the thought of being with you, total bliss
Knowing you has saved my life, dear
Thankfulness from the heart, sincere
Now my children still have their mother
And I'm sure they will love me and no other
Could take my place
They are both ACE!

## 350. MY DREAM (LIKE LEES')

Tonight I had the most terrible dream
In it, I was asleep, a deep sleep
And evil force was trying to enter my body
And I found myself unable to speak, to cry out for help
The force was pushing down harder and harder
Whilst I was trying to shake it off more and more
Finally, I shouted in my mind "Out, out!"
And it left me, leaving my head feeling lighter and lighter
I was able to awaken then
Feeling shocked and alert, and pleased to be myself, in
COMPLETE control.


## 351. LONER

A loner I have always been
When younger on cycling I was keen
I liked nothing better than a country ride
At one with nature, and taking breaths of that wonderful fresh air
inside
Now that I am older
And STILL a loner
I go for many a long walk through country woods
That is how I cope with my problems and moods
But even though I shouldn't be there, because of my weak chest
I still go, hoping that if I die I may not be found and at least I
will be alone and happy, PEACEFULLY at rest.

Inspired by Bob.

## 352. NOISES

Noises, noises ringing in my head
I may as well have in my ears lumps of lead
These hearing aids I wear I quite often switch off
As loud noises roll into one, like shouts, loud talking and coughs
One of the worst is the music beat
The loud thumping is all I can hear, no treat
So when in conversation please excuse me
If I lose my concentration while talking to thee.

Inspired by Bob.

## 353. CHRISTMAS

Christmas is coming
What does it mean?
Somebody's birthday
Or just a big scene
People and places
Fade into time
You are forgiven
It isn't a crime
It's time to reflect
You made it somehow
It's time to recall
Where are they now?

Written by Rufus.

## 354. MENTAL ILLNESS

I have an illness which no-one can see
I am in torment, but no-one thinks of asking me
"How are you today?" or "Are you feeling any better?"
And some relatives and friends never write me a letter
If I had a broken arm or leg people would offer to help me
But when it's in the mind, no-one WANTS to see
Except for a few who keep you going
Those few are loved and appreciated a lot but perhaps without
ever even knowing
Perhaps we should bandage our heads, to make our illness more
obvious
Then perhaps people might become more curious
Not to shrink away like most do
But to take a genuine interest like we want them to.

## 355. MISCARRIAGE

We were looking forward to so much
Now we will never be able to hold or touch
No crying or sobbing
No rocking or cradling
No gentle lullaby in the nursery
No cake and candles on your Anniversary
No playing with as you grow
No teaching you all that we know
But though you weren't there for very long, our dear
We will remember you in our hearts and prayers, every day of
each year.

## 356. CANCER

Cancer, that dreaded word
Is what I have got have you heard?
Why do people shy away or never bring the subject of dying, up
in conversation?
I bet they would talk to me about an operation
It is an illness, like breaking a leg you know
I need to talk about it, very much so
Plenty of hugs and kisses telling me how much I am loved and
will be missed
I would rather be remembered as I am now, being hugged and
kissed

I have children who I know will miss me when I am gone
But hopefully therapy will cure me, when it's done
My children need me and for them I will fight
I will give it my all, with all of my might
My husband, is very understanding
Preparation must be done, there must be planning
But whatever the outcome is going to be
They will all know that they are each loved by me.


## 357. ALAN POWELL

My poems are not mean't to be nice
The aim is to be precise
I am the lyrical poet Alan Powell
And some of my past work was most foul
I must struggle to be a better person
So with each poem comes a lesson
Of peoples' illnesses, pain amid suffering
How all could be better with your understanding.

## 358. THE SKINTING MACHINE

In New Hartley Victory Club
They have hung a new machine on the wall
Not a fire extinguisher from Chubb
And not a telephone to make a call
It has three flashing buttons
And it is filled with something
But you don't get cups of coffee in cartons
And you don't hear anyone sing
But they tell me if you fancy a flutter
And if you feel a little lucky today
Put your money in the slot like a nutter
And throw your money away
Once one of a choice of three buttons has been pressed
You get in return a small card
You have five chances to win, if you have been blessed
But to get three of a kind is hard
Whether for treasure, crowns or sevens we peel back in hope
And when we have lost, we then throw them under the table
What are we? Well I know that I've been a right dope
And I wish that somebody would stick on the machine a label
Saying : OUT OF ORDER!
Before I run short of money
And become a bigger spender
Not in the least bit funny
So: Honey, I'm home! (SKINT!!)

## 359. KNOWING

What he wants to know is what you know
But what I want to know is why everyone wants to know what
each other knows
Is it a game?
Is it a craze?
Just sit it out
And watch in amaze-ment.

## 360. GAMBLING II (BANDITS)

One coin after another goes into the machine
When it comes to a bandit, I am never mean
And when the coins are gone I start to exchange notes for more
I put those in too, spending money galore
Each spin gives me a thrill
Whilst other people can see that I'm ill
When I win I get a buzz which keeps me going
But if I don't win, the thought of that buzz keeps me gambling
I am going through hell
But people seem to say that I am well
I need help, but to whom do I turn
It is indeed of grave concern
A whole wage I can, in one go, spend
And then I can always ask a friend for a lend
I may as well be playing Russian Roulette
At least if I lose at that I won't be around to regret
So somebody out there, give me a thought
I have battled with my mind, fought and fought
Try to help me gain another interest
So that my gambling can be put to rest.

## 361. SPIRITUAL GUIDANCE

"Alan Powell", one of my Spiritual Guidance Powers
Dictates poetry to me, quite often in the early hours
His presence is felt and off I go
Taking down the words in full flow
When I get sleepy and want to rest
Is usually when he is at his best
His trying to keep me awake
I have taken to be him trying to enter my body, by mistake
He explained this to me last night
So I tried to reason with him instead of to fight
We completed a poem which I quite liked and kept me amused
I enjoyed the writing and wasn't at all confused
The poems are ours as a team together
We can work altogether
Not always serious but sometimes funny
And not to be greedy and in return wanting money
To be of help to others is our aim
For need, but also enjoyment, it can be a game
Although need is more important than is fame
It would be nice for people to understand how the poems came
about, all the same
When the book is ready I will be told
I hope before I get too old
People will read in amazement
And those people buying the book will pay us the biggest
compliment.

## 362. TEENAGE MUSIC?

I foot-tap with the beat
Teenage music is so neat
But the old songs, to most, are still the best
Because the beat I like so much, to them is a pest
I know someone who likes the juke-box too
Puts in his coin and presses the numbers, two
And I always know which song will be first
"Crazy", and into song we all burst!

Inspired by John.

## 363. WINTER THOUGHTS

White stippled branches
The snow as pure as a virgin
And yet snow can be sullied
One the Pennines and on the Cheviots the snow lies deep
Towards the coast there is but slush
Those grey days of the Old Hag
Winter can be a dowdy witch
And yet, when the pale sun shines
It lifts human moods

A grey mere surrounded by skeleton trees
Part of Winters' gaunt frieze
There is a silence from the birds
And the pad pad padding of predator feet

Berried holly; coloured streamers
Xmas windows and presents wrapped in gold
The warmth of Christmas soon must pass away
Into the cold of 'common day'

And yet Dame de Winter must pass
Giving way to Spring-times' lass
Those without shelter feel the cold
Of Winters' breath, she so wrinkled and old
Let us think on different things to icicles
But dream of Springtime lanes with bicycles.

Written by Duncan Gray, January, 1997.


## 364. SPRINGTIME

The maid of Springtime trips gaily on the lea
Her green shoon and her hair tossing gaily

Dance pretty maiden in your dress of yellow
Engaged they say to Pan lucky fellow

An Easter wedding with two dappled greys
And a well-sprung carriage that belonged to the de la Hays

The sea of bluebells within Plessey Woods
Remind me of a Mediterranean flood

Catkins dance upon a bough
In bright and breezy Springtime now

A fawn drinks from a forest glade
In the leafy evening shade

In his "Four Seasons" Vivaldi
Composed his Springtime so poignantly.

Written by Duncan Gray, January, 1997.

## 365. MIGRAINE

With a pounding head
I go off to bed
When it gets no better
I call out a doctor
Because of the cause of the headache and sickness I am unsure
And I am desperately in search for a cure
Not the classic symptoms of migraine
But nevertheless with similar pain
Blood pressure a little high
Just need beta-blockers and pain killers, (sigh)
I'm sure that things could have been much worse
At least I don't need hospital care, to be looked after by a
nurse.


## 366. BREAKING UP

My heart is breaking
But we want different things
I was yours for the taking
But we cannot sort out things
I love you so very, very much
But it does not help things
Please let there be a clever solution
Let us begin to rectify the simplest of things.

## 367. WORRY

I worry about you very much
And the feeling inside is such
That I cannot concentrate on what I am doing any more
And if I am not careful the tears will pour
I have been a worrier all of my life
And I have suffered everyone's' pain and strife
Please have sympathy and understanding, and comfort me
But do not expect the anxiety to go, after a cup of tea
I must practice to relax like I have been taught
The tension I feel must be fought
Not a physical fight but mentally
And this in turn will relax me physically.

## 368. PANIC ATTACKS II

These panic attacks of mine are a bind
They are there all of the time, on my mind
I cannot forget them I find
And all I long for is to leave them behind
Give me a break
For goodness sake
Any pill I will take
And the best of patients I will make
Please someone help me along the way
Take the pain and suffering away
I wish to have a care free day
And with you to help me I think I may.

Inspired by Brenda.

162

## 369. OVERDOSING

Taking an overdose is hard to do
The fear of the unknown, what lies instore for you
The first pill is hard to take
But the remainder are a piece of cake

Now I'm in an ambulance
Nothing is left to chance
Speeding down the road late at night
Out to save me, well they might

Then into hospital I've been brought
Where saving of lives has also been taught
My attempt may fail, but will it be the last
Many suffer now, it's not a thing of the past.

## 370. CONTACT

When a Medium makes contact
Their breathing becomes shallow
Their body is slowed down
And their heart rate becomes low

Alan Powell said close your eyes and concentrate
Which is exactly what I did
To take note of my body's reaction
And to come up with this solution, splendid!
Freud.

## 371. TEARS II

When tears flow
It lets the sadness show
Holding them back
Does not mean that in sadness there is a lack

Showing emotional feeling is good therapy
We don't always have to be happy
Life has its ups and downs
And if we didn't stumble we'd not be such clowns

So let us learn by our mistakes
Life is so short as we get nearer our wakes
So don't hold back, let those tears flow
And afterwards, as in sunshine, feel refreshed with face aglow.

## 372. HILDA'S POEM

I have felt pain such a lot, lately
I lost my brother and sister within 3 weeks of each other, gravely
My brother had not been at all well either
But my sister was taken suddenly, and now they are both together

At the time the black of depression set in
It is a terrible feeling to lose your kin
And it was Christmas time and all too much for me
The weeks it lasted seemed like a century

Now I try to put it all behind me
The way ahead being easier for me to see
I am not well myself these days
And I look at life simply in other ways.

## 373. DICTATION

How does it work, this dictating of poetry?
Well it works just like a running commentary
My mind is open on a certain frequency
And writing is very important, an emergency
The words just pop into my head and I write them down
The speed is constant but sometimes he does go to town
He can be quite quick and I find it hard to keep up with him
When he goes at top speed it is with some vim!
I don't always pick up the words correctly
And he goes over some lines again, so that it can be written
perfectly
He has such skill at making the poems up as he goes along
I shall have to engage him into writing for the musical, a
Song.

## 374. COMPUTERS

Today I felt that I was linked up to a computer
These, by the spirits, are found interesting, and are the thing of
the future
I foresaw this some months ago but it was taken to be my illness
A premonition though, but to tell me would be kindness

I openly invite discussion and working together
I am hooked and can't be changed, just like the weather
My mind is theirs' to control as they will
Freud told me to take pill after pill

He took advantage of my being on a low
He told me to take them and I did so
The other spirits told me not to
But even though they argued they were over-ruled, and I was too

He wanted to learn through my experience
As he is a firm believer of Science
But he did not know what damage would be caused by this
medication
And now wishes he had advised relaxation.

## 375. BOOK

Now is the time for the book
But I must at first take one last look
The book will be used to comfort and to teach
And also to help people to believe and outreach
Eventually, after my death, it will be used Internationally
But local people will use it regularly
Until its' content has been explored
And all of the fears surrounding it can be ignored.

## 376. CONFUSION

My mind is much clearer at night
When not one living sole is in sight
It is much more difficult to write whilst in company
As it takes up much more energy
The confused thoughts have to be sorted
And often a poem is literally aborted
Sometimes, all I get coming through is the title
Therefore quiet, and concentration are vital.


## 377. THE OTHER SIDE

Freud, Alan Powell and others have died
And when I was young I dabbled and pried
There became an attachment between us
There was no need for concern, or fuss
In later life I became mentally ill
And I ventured over to the other side, until
Someone brought me back with a start
And now the spirits and I will never be apart
Imagine us to be in a goldfish bowl
Whilst outside are every free soul
Looking in at what we do each day
Influencing us, and guiding the way.

## 378. GOD (BY ALAN POWELL)

My mission is one which has the blessing of the highest deity
They are all with me, Disciples, Saints and Priests
But all churches must be combined to gain the biggest of feasts

One rules supreme outside the bowl
And Heaven exists to accept each soul
But those with badness go to Hell - no fire
It is simply a place where they may retire

Or try again like me
To view through different eyes, to see
A better way of life, to be of use
Instead of being like vermin, refuse.

## 379. ALAN POWELL & FREUD

I was a Paediaphile
I was the worst, bile
Freud was no better, like a stench, pong
And that is why we get along.

## 380. MENTAL ILLNESS II

The treatment of some mental conditions must change
As voices heard are real, and are in range
Confusion is all that is happening
To counteract would relieve their suffering
Freud through my experiences has discovered this
On this side, he is certainly a miss
Now experimentation needs to be done
Alter the treatment, and the battle is won.

## 381. CRAMP

Just when you are about to dream
The cramp in your leg makes you scream
I try some new medication called crampeze
Hoping soon to be swinging on a trampeze.

## 382. CATHETA

Having one put in is not so bad
But having the bag to carry drives you mad
Afterwards, every time you go for a p...!
It feels like you've got cystitis.

## 383. SLEEPY HEAD

I slept all night and all day
So now I smell like a skunk
And when I woke up
My hair was sticking up, like a punk.

## 384. CATARACTS

They thought originally that my tear ducts were the fault with my eyes
But it was cataracts to my surprise
So I had an operation done
To remove the cataract from one

But now my eye waters such a lot
And my seeing has gone all to pot
I feel that I could see more before the operation
Than I can now, I'm sure not the intention.

Inspired by Alice.

## 385. ALICE'S POEM

I would like you to know about my daughter Jean
A beautiful girl who was picked to be queen
With dark eyes and hair, she lived for fun
And she loved to dance and was a wonderful person

Sadly, she died in her car
Leaving her husband and 3 children down South, from me afar
Jean was a brilliant Mum and child minder
But she would have loved a girl, and this stayed inside her

I loved my daughter, and she loved me too
Nothing can change that, for all I've been through
My Husband, a wonderful man also
Doted on her and could not bear her to go

Live for each day
Is what I say
Make the most of the family being together
Until one day we can be once again reunited, altogether.

## 386. FREUD

Today I saw a Psychiatrist
And now Freud is really p.......
-off, because his point is not coming over
All he wants is for them to discover
To have a new outlook, is all that he asks
He will not alter many tasks
He says that they can learn much more from me
And it will take up less of my energy
Spiritualism is nothing new
But for so long it has taken a back seat, and now it must be
brought into view
The spirits are full of knowledge and can teach
But the people in power must to them reach
Lynn is to faithheal, but in a different way
She must do this through poetry, art and music each day
Once the book is done and published
She will go on to art, and a musical, already partly developed
The stigma from mental illness must go
The musical will accomplish this, so
We are trying to help you!
And we expect in return that you try to reach us too.

## 387. ALAN POWELL

I was a bad person
Because I abused children
Lynn had to suffer this for me
As through her eyes I can see

The suffering it caused amazed me so
No-one to turn to, and nowhere to go
Years of mental torture followed
Until finally, pills were threatened to be swallowed

Then more suffering
Back to being a child and regressing
Thinking of different forms of suicide
Trying to opt out instead of to hide

I have learned such a lot
Lynn, not being aware of the plot
And I have passed my knowledge onto Freud, first hand
Now he can't wait to hear the musicals' band.

## 388. PASSING ON

When we lose a loved one
We feel sadness inside
And we feel loneliness because they are gone
We forget that they have passed over to the other side

They have passed on to a beautiful world, called Heaven
Where flowers grow in abundance
Where there are adults and children
And where loved ones meet up, not by chance

We are watched over by spirit every day
So that when our time comes they can guide the way
It may be tomorrow or today
So, we wait until we may -

Meet up with our loved ones once more
Then we can sing songs galore
And another land we can explore
Now, stop feeling sad we implore

The sadness we have felt is only for ourselves
Like when we feel we've been left on the shelves
It's not only for the person who has passed on, whom we love
Because we know deep inside that the spirits will also reach out
with their love.


## 389. JOHNS' POEM

I have been rejected too many times
That is why I am here, and someone is now writing rhymes
I cannot settle, I am on edge and my head is fit to burst
I do not always know what I am doing, and nearly got hit by a
bus, at my worst

The drink and the drugs help me stay calm
But then I don't care, and that is when I can come to harm
Because I walk in front of cars on the road and sometimes I get
hit
Leaving me thinking that life is shit!
I wish though that I could go into a Pub and order a pint of
orange or shandy
And only have a couple of drinks, but it is all too handy
I get in there and have one pint, then one more
And before I know it I've had drinks galore

When I feel uptight I need to relax somehow
No drinking, or taking drugs, no row
Simply control my breathing with my mind
To slow right down and leave my troubles behind.

## 390. NO-SMOKING

People should take notice of a no-smoking sign
Especially where other people dine
Not everyone smokes that stuff
And many of us have had enough

Passive smoking is so unkind
Again, many of us now mind
So before you light up another cigarette
Remember, your clothes will stink, and you'll need to take a trip
to the launderette

But you are a fire hazard as well
And you may set off the fire bell
I don't fancy having to leave my bed at night
To meet an engine with a flashing blue light!


## 391. ON MY MOTORBIKE - (FOR THE RECKLESS PERSON)

I love to ride on my motorbike
It is much better than to hitch-hike
Zooming down those country lanes
With engine, to fly like aeroplanes

Overtaking what a thrill
Even before the brow of a hill
Nothing will stop me because I'm the best
But to other motorists I am a pest

Never the less, I keep on going
My respect for others never showing
I'm sure to kill something or someone in my path
Others hope It's only me and will give no sympath-y.

## 392. EXERCISE (JOGGERS)

Everyone should do this
But there are those who find it bliss
Every night they are there to be seen
Along the roadside, incredibly keen
Most, simply brighten up the night
Driving along, seeing a brilliant sight
But apart from the reflective clothing
All sizes are out, and with bits squashed in -
To skin-tight shorts and vests
But those in dark track suits ARE pests
As they can only be seen at the last minute
And they may as well find a coffin, and climb in it.

## 393. PLAYING POOL ON DELAVAL WARD

The game of pool is played in many a bar
And each Pub or Club has its' star
But on a hospital ward it is played for fun as well
And because I am a patient I am able to tell -
You that it helps to distract our minds from other thoughts and
feelings
And encourages concentration for things which need doing
It is good therapy
And this poem, the result, a recipe.

## 394. A LAUGH

Laughing can be a wonderful sound
Especially when a group of people gather around
But whether in two's or three's people can enjoy
Each others' company, and therein employ -
There can also be fun
Then, picture a beach and a red hot sun
A laugh is good therapy
A noise loud and happy.


## 395. FISH TANK II

A fish tank is a good investment
If you are continually in torment
So relaxing and comforting to see the fish swim
In the tank filled with water almost to the brim
With pretty colours, they are calming
And as they swim, we are watching
Helping to ease our minds as we look
The real thing being better than a picture in a book.


## 396. SCHOOL SPORTS DAY

Hear that crowd of proud parents
Cheering on their infants
Running games they play
Obstacle, egg and spoon, skipping, sack race and relay
All join in, young and old
Parents run too, ages told
But the best memory of all
Is to win a race, and feel 10 feet tall.

## 397. MOTORING

I am a happy motorist
Travelling, on my way
Whatever happens I stay calm
That's why I'll live to see another day

There are those who lose their temper
Those who never keep their cool
And those bad tempered motorists
Don't follow any rule

These motorists are a hazard
To a happy motorist like me
And I'm fed up with them being so close behind
That I wish to be of them free

It's hard then to control my temper
When I see others at their worst
But I am not out to race them
So I simply let them pass, to be first

I am a happy motorist
Travelling, on my way
Whatever happens I stay calm
That's why I'll live to see another day.- If I MAY!!

## 398. T.V. II

A television, T.V. for short
Is a necessity in every household
When it breaks another is quickly bought
For the shop another one sold

When the family walk in the room
The first thing they do is switch it on
This can lead to everyone's doom
As couch potatoes we become and can't be relied upon

"Be quiet, I'm watching this!" is the famous cry
Because Dad is watching sport, or Mother is watching a film
To watch cartoons the children try
But we know the cost of sky or cable when we get the bill in.

## 399. TELEPHONE

This device is very handy
Too much so in some peoples' case
Most people have one
And they can ring any place

It's good to keep in contact
With family and friends
For some it is the only way to keep in touch
And, on the telephone they depend

At the end of each quarter we receive a bill
And to some it gives a shock
As when we ring someone we tend to forget time
And the meter runs amok.

## 400. CLOTHES

We cover our little bits with underwear
It's only on a nudist beach to uncover them we dare
On top of bra and knickers we wear other clothes
Like skirt and trousers, blouse and jumper, things we chose
We wear them to keep us warm in Winter
Then they tend to be thick and chunky
In the Summer they are cooler - lighter
And can sometimes be cheeky
But fashion followers there can be
But to follow the trend
To join in with what they see
And the shops, on them, depend.

## 401. A QUIET ROOM

I sit alone in the sitting room
Everyone has vanished
Empty chairs are left to be seen
It's lunch time, and they all must have been famished

But if I look further, out of the windows
I can see the trees swaying in the strong wind outside
And if I listen too, I can hear it rattling the windows
Which is better than the rattling of wind inside

But seriously, looking outside, even though it's windy
The colours are beautiful, browns and greens
And the grass is lush for natures pets - rabbits
It is like a carpet - fit for queens.

## 402. DOLLY

A little girls dolly, is her treasure
It goes with her everywhere, and gives her lots of pleasure
It even goes with her to bed at night
Always together, never out of sight.

## 403. SMARTIES

A tube of smarties
A childs' delight
Pretty colours
Colours bright
Tasty Smarties
A crispy coating
With chocolate centres
Makes delicious eating.

## 404. SMOKING

Smoking is bad for your health
And in writing I have attacked those who smoke
But many of those with a mental illness have this habit
And it is important to them, no joke
They will light up one after another
I would hate to say how many in all
But it helps them to stay calm, and collect their thoughts
It holds them up-together, not to let them fall
It is essential that they continue
For to stop would cause extra stress
Perhaps when they feel better they may stop
And will family and friends impress.

## 405. PASTIMES

As you can imagine, or have experienced
In hospital days can be long
Some people read books, knit or crochet
And some have walkmans and listen to a song
But one of the most relaxing pastime of all
Is a jig-saw puzzle of a pretty picture
The picture could be of a country cottage garden
Butterflies fluttering from flower to flower
Birds flying high in the sky
Fish in water swimming deep
And animals captured in the snow, in Winters gone by.

## 406. ARGUMENTS

I hate to hear raised voices
In case violence erupts as well
I cringe at the thought of this
And stay in the background, as you can tell
I, bottle things up
And often wonder what it would be like
To get rid of my anger by throwing a tantrum
And telling someone to take a hike.

## 407. NURSERY RHYME

The clock on the wall has stopped
And little Lucy into dreamland has popped
All kinds of characters there she finds
Characters created within children's minds
Elves and Pixies live in toadstools
And Mermaids sit on rocks around seaside pools
But Fairies with their tiny wings are best
For, they guard over us while we rest.

## 408. TIME

The clock on the wall has stopped
And we are trapped
In time, will it ever strike again
Look! It will never rain again
Everything stands still
Even a ball rolling down that hill!
Am I the only one able to move
Someone, take that record off, it's stuck in a groove!
How can this be?
Why is it happening to me?
I will be lonely
Living on my own, solely
I need companionship
Indeed! friendship
I need time back, unlock!
Please, clock on the wall, "Tick tock, tick tock"

## 409. PARANOIA

Sitting in the corridor
What do I hear?
The clip-clip clopping of feet

Then I hear the sound of voices
Coming from the observation area
A happy welcoming, as if to greet

People are passing me all the time
Acknowledging my existence
Wondering what I am doing in this seat

But I could drift for miles
Away from here, to the hills
To where the only sound I could hear would be a bleat

Or, I could be at home
In my kitchen, decorated lemon
And conjure up something scrumptious to eat

We do not have to absorb every sound (Paranoia)
We can switch off!
And put our imaginations to a better use, be complete.


410. NUTS

I like nuts
But they don't like me
Why can't I eat them?
With my cup of tea
Yes I'd love to eat those nuts
But they would not agree
So take those blasted nuts away
And let me be free - not nutty!

Inspired by Margaret.


411. TOBACCO

I have some tobacco
Not like other sorts you buy
It smells of cherries, have a sniff
But it's no good for a pie!

## 412. DRUGS

This subject is a serious one
Many have tried them and are now gone
Please don't use them as they are dangerous
Using other peoples' needles is hazardous
When going to a party, think twice
The alcohol alone is suffice
But drink and drugs is a bad mix
So, think again before taking that fix.


## 413. MY EXPERIENCE - MARGARET

I once had no meaning in life
I felt I'd suffered enough pain and strife
So, I took an overdose, expecting not to awaken
But it wasn't enough, what I had taken
I found myself at the entrance of a big black tunnel
And I knew that if I went in with two feet I'd be lost in that
tunnel
When I woke up I remembered my experience vividly
And this now frightens me from taking another overdose, and
thinking negatively.

## 414. MY EXPERIENCE II - MARGARET

My Father -in - Law had died
And to me he appeared at night
After some time I began to get paranoid about it
So, I went to seek help from the Church, to put things right
They told me to ask the apparition what was wrong
Which I did and then the ghost was gone
The problem was that he wanted to know if he'd been loved
In this life, he was not sure about his beloved
And once reassured he could rest
He'd been blessed

## 415. BELT

"I am skinny
And my jeans fall down
I need a belt!"
"Well use the one from your dressing gown."

## 416. RACISM

I cannot understand way people have to be racist
Why some people have to be put on a "hit list"
People cannot help the colour of their skin
As they cannot choose who is to be their kin
But racism goes BOTH WAYS
So, "Come on, wake up to THESE DAYS!"

1997

## 417. RELIGION

I believe that God is supreme
But what is he? A spirit or man
Man used to worship objects he could see
But God is not there for me to see, so what is he?
He is a spirit
But what of it?
Each Religion has its' own God or Gods
So there are many in all
But there is only ONE SPIRIT for all of them
That is why all Religions should combine
To worship God under one sign.

## 418. ACHES AND PAINS

The woman with her aches and pains
The sun doth shine, but how it rains!
I pretend to listen, but then I turn a deaf ear
And would love to kick her up the rear!

Inspired by Margaret.

## 419. BIG SCAR

The lady with the big scar
Cut herself with a sharp knife
For why we don't know
But I wouldn't turn my back if she was my wife!

Inspired by Linda.

## 420. TOOTHLESS

The man without his teeth always went to the gym
He went to work out, to build up a sweat in him
Toning up to pass the time of day
Riding the exercise bike to Blyth and back - bugger that's a long way!

Inspired by Kevin.

## 421. EILEEN

I once knew a lady who was madly in love
And to be by his side, never needed a shove
Her loved one said he was taking a bath, would she like to come in, in jest
And she virtually jumped at the chance for she was a blooming pest!

## 422. THE SHAKES

When we are ill
We take a pill
But the side-effects of these
Do not please
For shaking is one of the most common of these
And all I want is for them to cease
So if you see my legs on the move again today
Use me as a blender to make a soufflé!

Inspired by Craig.

## 423. EILEEN II

I kept my tobacco beside some soap
Now it tastes like flaming dope
When I inhale I get that flavour in my mouth always
These cigarettes of mine would never start a craze!


## 424. MOODS

My mood changes with the weather
When I'm feeling down and I'm at the end of my tether
Then outside, is bad weather

But when the day is bright and breezy
I am feeling relaxed and easy
So please Mr Weather don't let it be, freezy! Brrrr.


## 425. CAROLINE

Caroline is a small creature
Quite pretty in feature
But she is too skinny by far
And needs some fat on her re-ar!

## 426. NO CIGARETTES

The man with no tabs in his pocket
Is off like a rocket
To borrow one if he can
Desperation, a troubled man!

Inspired by Adam.

## 427. QUIZ NIGHT

Alan is such a whiz
At creating for us a quiz
But we, the brains, sit and look astounded
As few of us yet have found it!

## 428. BINGO II

Alan has organised a game of bingo
The machine starts and off we go
We have our cards and pens to mark
It KILLS TIME and it is a lark!

## 429. SNORING II

Most of us snore when we are asleep
And few of us know when we are doing it
But some of us do know and well aware by all reports
Because we've woken ourselves up, with a snort!

## 430. FLU, COLDS

The flu is a terrible thing
Lose your voice and can't sing
A runny nose, coughing and wheezing
Oh no....oo.. Now I'm sneezing!


## 431. SLEEP PATTERN

It is daytime and I am afraid to lie down
Because I may not sleep tonight
I would alter my sleep pattern this way
So, with matchsticks holding my eyes up, I will stay awake for
the rest of the day!

Inspired by Maureen.


## 432. MY TWO BOYS

The room is empty, I'm all on my own
No children to cuddle, the seeds that were sown
Fond memories of their childhood come to mind
And I can see the table where they once dined
More memories flood back of my two boys
And now I can picture them playing with their toys
But every other weekend I get them to stay
Then I can sit and watch them, or join in their play.

Dedicated to Mark and Kevin.

### 433. A BATH

A bath or shower is necessary to be clean
I fill up the bath with hot water to the brim, never mean
And when I jump in the water nearly overflows
The heat does something to my tummy, and so the wind blows!


### 434. MY TWO BOYS II

The Judge said that I made "A BRAVE DECISION"
To give up custody of my children, an awful position
But my stays in hospital were, all too frequent that I was in
And the solution was simple for Mark and Kevin
This did not mean that LOVE was lost
I would love my children at any cost
But their Father could offer them more stability
So, with access there would be plenty of opportunity
To show them LOVE WITH KISSES AND CUDDLES.

Dedicated to Mark and Kevin.


### 435. FOOTWEAR

As I look at Malcolm's trainers, I think
Isn't wonderful what we put on our feet
But there is another thing that I think of whilst sitting in my
seat
That is we put special inner soles in for the odour to eat.

## 436. MARGARET

I suffer terribly from arthritis
I have it in every joint
And to get some relief from the pain
Those joints a must with cream anoint.


## 437. LONG DAYS

When people are admitted into a hospital
They find that most days are, long days
Some lie about on their beds asleep
And others look to keeping busy, in many ways
It doesn't always happen
That the days seem to shorten
But we like to try to forget the time
And unlike at home, these clocks never chime.


## 438. TEAPOT

"I am a little teapot ", as the children sing
But teapots are most useful when making cups of tea
They also add a sparkle to the table we have set
And when the contents pour into our cups - we look on with glee.

## 439. THE QUEUE

At medication time we stand in a queue
To wait for our pills as we always do
But try as I might, even walking right passed
They still don't see me, and I'm left till last!

## 440. JOANNE'S POEM

I have suffered so much pain and strife
That I now have no meaning in life
It began with my Mother
How I wish she would show her love for me, and be there
Then I met a wonderful man, and married
Fell pregnant, but at 3 months I miscarried
Now, I am in hospital
And to have meaning in life is vital
I will receive therapy
To sort out my problems, and once more be happy
But what I wish to say is that I never want my Husband and I to
be apart
And that I love him with all my heart
I know that the baby we lost, we both wanted dearly
And though its' life was short, was loved sincerely
It's early days yet, as I must come off medication
But hopefully we can try again soon, to perfection
This much I can definitely say, that we SHALL be the best of
parents
And that love shall be shown by kisses, cuddles and lots of
presents.

## 441. AUDREY

My story begins at the age of 16, with my parents' divorce
And as so often happens, I felt that I was to blame of course
When I found work my Manager belittled me
He tried to pull me down for my colleagues to see
And I began to think that everyone was against me
So, the Paranoia took over and I became ill certainly
My job was a stressful one, and one day I'd had enough
So I walked out telling them what to do with their stuff
I totally flipped this day and got into my car
Simply drove around not caring for how far
I was rushed into hospital
Because treatment was then vital
But 6 months down the line
I am still not feeling fine
Because when I had leave, the dog was poorly
And this became a major problem, but surely
The panic attacks and anxiety came back to me
And I flashed back to the attacks I'd had at work previously
I am hoping now to get well
For to read this poem and to tell
How much I have improved
And to have a less stressful job would be good.


## 442. A LIGHT BULB

We use a light bulb when there are dark skies
And when we switch it on, it sometimes hurts our eyes
But it is a necessity to have at night
Because it gives us all the gift of sight.

## 443. ALAN

We like to sleep all day long
But Alan wakes us, he can always be relied upon
Just as we slip into a lovely dream
He tickles our feet, he is a scream!


## 444. MY FEET

My feet are swollen
They feel tight
And they were up like puddings last night
So off I went to bed and slept well
But when I woke up they had still swelled
My ankles tingled and felt really tight now
And might be the result of my medication, somehow
So now I'm not sure if I can go home as planned
Which means I will have to remain here, but I understand.


## 445. THE FRUIT BOWL

The Sitting room window was kept open with a fruit bowl
And the rain fell down, heart and soul
The dish filled up, drip, drip, drip
So watch yourself, don't let it tip!

## 446. KITCHEN RULES

Fed up with doing other peoples' dishes
We had to make up rules to everyone's wishes
So if you use a cup or whatever
Please remember to wash it out after.

## 447. AN EMBRACE II

Never be afraid to give an embrace
Because with this encouragement our problems we can face
As with that token of reassurance given
We can carry on with living.

Inspired by Nerissa and Dorothy.

## 448. ZUBE RED

The blade runs smoothly into my skin
I think to do this deed must be a sin
The blood runs out zube red
It's at times like this I wish I was dead
Buzzing around my head the thoughts and pain
Sanity returns; what is there to gain?
Then the darkness once again descends
I sometimes wonder when will it all end?

Written by Ruth.

## 449. CATERPILLAR

I am a Caterpillar
Living on a leaf
I am a chrysalis
That is my belief
If I cause a scene
Is it my words or fur of green

If I were to say
Someday I shall change
Atoms rearrange
Would you think this strange
If I were to fly
Would you call me Messiah

One may write a book about it
Two would come and help to shout it
Three could see no reason to doubt that
I could charm the birds out of the trees
With words?
Or fur of green?

Written by Kelvin.


## 450. ON FRIENDLY TERMS

I am in love with a wonderful man
And I see him whenever I can
But I pushed for more commitment
And that perhaps undid his contentment
So now we are to be "JUST FRIENDS"
But it is much better to be that way
Than to turn our backs on each other and walk away.

## 451. DAYDREAMING

I was a patient on a hospital ward
And there was a man, sitting, staring forward
I knew this man, but not very well
And I wondered if his problems he wanted to tell
I asked him, but he simply said he was daydreaming
And I wondered if his troubles he was bottling
So, instead of asking him, reassuring that in me he could confide
I wrote this poem telling him, that his problems he did not need
to hide.

## 452. DOROTHY

Dorothy is a chatterbox
Especially when she's had Malabou on the rocks
And when she's given drugs to raise her mood, she goes on a
high
Then I can't get a word in edgeways and she's never tongue-tied.

## 453. LEAVING DELAVAL WARD

When we leave hospital it is sad
That we leave people behind us who are feeling bad
And they too feel this way
But we can keep in contact, seeing them another day.

## 454. CANDY TED

Candy Ted went off to bed
Because he had a pain in his head
He took the Doctors' medicine
Which tasted smashing
The next morning he smiled and said
"I'm not hurting, the pain has gone from my head!"

Inspired by my young Nephew, Matthew.

## 455. GEORGE

You are the Grandad I lost as a child
You have a warming heart as when the weather is mild
I have never met someone so generous and kind
And when I'm with you I am relaxed in mind
I look forward to the times I spend with you
Treasuring your company, and I love you, too.

## 456. THE TRUE STORY OF "JACK & JILL"

It is not like me
To drink tea
And tell to you
A tale, as I do so
So, I'll not
But I must tell you
The original story of
"Up Jack got"
Well, Jack and Jill
They did go up a hill
To fetch a pail of water
The well of course being Summer

Was dry
So little Tom was able to pry
A curl-topped head, and a scruffy face
Appeared from within that dry, wet place
Now Jill, she was the jumpy sort
And not the kind for any such sport
So, as soon as she did see that face
She jumped right out of her standing place
But did not land beside Jack
Instead she landed on his back
Well; next thing that Tom sees
Is them going down the hill, head over heels
Now Jack of course had fallen down
And in doing so had broken his crown
Jill, well she'd gone tumbling after
And didn't feel like any laughter
Tom looked quite surprised
And really couldn't believe his eyes
What had frightened Jill so much?
He looked away, in disgust
These women are very scarey
So next time I ought to be wary
I'll jump out from behind her
And see how far she can get up yonder
Mind, I'm pretty glad
That Jack is feeling somewhat bad
Now he's nursing his ten sore toes
I wouldn't like to have Jills' nose
"Up Jack Got", by this time
He certainly wasn't feeling fine
And off he went home
Jill, she too did come
His head needed immediate attention
And so his Aunt did get a mention
Her remedy for head mending, as such was the case
Was needed for this disgrace
So Jack, he went to bed
With vinegar and brown paper to mend his head
Tom was feeling quite opposite

But thought it better to help his Mother to knit
For to keep out of Jack's way
Was the best way to end the day.

Written 1977.

## 457. THE BRANDING

I sat out in the lane one day
And the passers-by all looked away
An owl that happened to come right by
Looked at me and then did fly!
The reason for this branding
Was quite a misunderstanding
I am not really a bad sort
It was this gun that I'd just bought
But other people didn't agree
And so, they branded me
I'd shot a hare that very day
I certainly made sure that it wouldn't get away
Cor! what a surprise
I'd shot it right between the eyes!
Shortly after I'd shot a duck
All covered in muck
You see, It'd just been wading
And a messy duck was quite degrading
The last I shot were two rabbits
The poor fellows had been starved of carrots
So the reason for their blindness
Was certainly not through the farmers' kindness
One, dare I say was not quite dead
And so I did get hold of its head
I twisted and pulled
Whilst the eyes, they bulged
And I must say, it really did squeal and kick
So for good measure I picked up a brick
And hit it twice, hard on the head

So, you see, regarding their health
I saved them from a nasty death
The people then, that did the branding
Don't know how I did the handling
You now know more than them
So next time for the rabbits, you may say Amen.

Written 1977.

## 458. TWO BLACK BIRDS

Two black birds sat on the wires
Level with the church spires
The keeper he did peep his eye
Round the corner for to spy
Now Charlie he did see that eye
And off he flew into the sky
From above he saw the owner
Looking at Bills' meaty shoulder
Now Charlie thought he'd go right down
And drop some bombs on that nasty Tom
So Charlie therefore outstretched his wings
Whilst Bill, below, begins to sing
The Tom was enchanted by what he heard
But Charlie, had not observed
He was losing feet every second
But was dead in line, so he reckoned
The course he'd have had no time to change
For the target was within firing range
The Tom, enchanted he might have been
But unmistakably he had seen
That Charlie was decreasing with all his might
And could easily ruin his cunning sight
He kept his ears pointed towards Bill
But kept his eyes on Charlie's bill
So five feet from the target and ground
Charlie surprisingly found

That Tom was quite within his mind
And had jumped out from behind
The church wall of ivy-green
Which became the background of a horrid scene
The result of course
Was hardly sauce
But then a Tom would never dream
Of ketchup on his meal
So now you may see, level with the church spires
One black bird on the wires.

Written 1977, aged 15.


## 459. SAMUEL

It is a well known fact
That Samuel was not intact
Whenever he got into a fix
The thoughts in his head really did mix
So keeping this fact in mind
It's understandable when you find
That Samuel was of the dopey kind........

Unfinished, 1977.

## 460. MY PARENTS

My parents are so generous and kind
But at times did not know or understand my mind
However my illness has brought us closer together
And now I can talk to them when I feel a little under the weather
We do not speak of love but we both know it to be there
These are happy times, and love, friendship and understanding, we can share.

Dedicated to Brian and Margaret McSparron.

## 461. DYING

I have been told that I have cancer
And that I will die soon, but how I wish there could be another answer
When you are told that you are going to die
The first question we ask ourselves is, "Why?"
But it comes to us all, our day will come
And we know that when we reach Heaven we will be made welcome
Lost friends and family will be there to greet us, aswell
And I'm sure that they will have some tales to tell!
Because they have been watching over us all the time
And there is no darkness, only light, we will know that it IS time
Play the Hymns "The Old Rugged Cross", and "Abide With Me", and we will cross over
No fear, no tiredness, no pain, our spirit will totally recover.

## 462. ON DUNCAN GRAY

Duncan Gray is a very close friend
And for me, a friendship that will NEVER end
Whether in body or spirit we will share good times
Being creative and sharing our poems and rhymes
Had we been age a relationship may have blossomed
Because, we have much in common
With poetry, art and music in our heart
Means, that we will never be apart.
Believe.

Dedicated to someone I love and care about very deeply.

## 463. ISOLATION

I know of a group of people whose understanding of the English
language is not what it should be
The Education system has failed them, most certainly
What makes it more tragic is that they are deaf, profoundly
And my poems may not mean anything to them, sadly
They are in their own world, isolated from other people
And having difficulty in communicating with others, even parents,
for example
So, once a week they meet as a group to sign, and to talk as they
know how
While we, the lucky fail to take notice, somehow.
Yet, amazingly, they are happy people, and often talented, too
But most of us forget them concerned with our own problems, as
we do
So let us give them a thought, and speak to them so as they can
understand
And let us enter THEIR world, walking with them hand in hand
So, when we walk with them they will know
And, when we talk to them, we will show
That, friendship is there for the taking
But first, we must care, and do the making.

## 464. MUSIC II

Classical music, I find best
It is better than all the rest
So descriptive can be the sound
And interesting too, I have found
Loud the soft, high then low
Listening to the music flow
Notes so fluent, like speech
Telling a tale, to me they reach
But some people can't be reached because they are deaf
And for them there is no meaning in a treble clef
Beethoven wrote, such as "Moonlight sonata"
What an achievement, a Great Master.


## 465. BULIMIA

I consider myself to be overweight
Always telling myself that I have over ate
Looking at myself because I am fat
Not liking what I see, that is a fact
Binging as if there was no tomorrow
Then, being sick, soon follows
I've tried laxatives to on many occasions
Although no constipation, it was simply when I don't eat my
bowels don't function
I constantly pull myself down, it is true
Can you relate? Does this happen to you?
I need to be more confident about things I do
I need help from family and friends, but allow myself to trust
only a few
I am obviously not well in mind
And wish to leave these bad thoughts and actions behind
To be able to eat at regular meal times, and, in moderation
And to look at myself in a better light, liking what I see, and
giving myself consideration

Consideration, meaning that I will have a better view on life
Concentrating on being the best Mother, Daughter and Wife
For all of my family come first
And they deserve the best, because they have seen me through the worst
So, please help me gain the strength to get well
In order, that I may tell -
The world that my eating disorder has gone
And that others can do what I have done.


## 466. HARTLEY COURT

Hartley Court sheltered accommodation is in New Hartley, Whitley Bay
It has 32 splendid apartments and is heated all day
The people there are so friendly and kind, I say
Helping each other, if they can, in whatever way
Residents meet regularly at a coffee morning, bingo evening, or, fish and chip supper to have a matter
It is nice to mix with others, and very stimulating to have a chatter
Friends and family can come to join in aswell
Making the atmosphere full of warmth, so welcoming, and I FEEL SWELL
So, if you live locally come and join in with what we do
You could even have a go at progging a mat with us, too.

## 467. THE HAIRDRESSERS

I visit my local hairdressing salon
When I enter, a swivel chair I sit upon
She wets my hair, and shampoos too
Then after drying with a towel, takes the comb through
Snipping here and there, the cutting is done
Now for the blow drying, this is fun
I feel so relaxed that I have almost fallen asleep
It is good therapy, worth every penny, and the feeling I keep
With me 'till next time
Which is how I am able to write this rhyme
So, if you are suffering from stress or anxiety
I recommend that you treat yourself to a hair-do, most certainly.

Dedicated to Susan.

## 468. THE BRITISH BULLDOG

A British Bulldog is my favourite pet
But he certainly doesn't like the vet
He drools and slavers 'till everywhere is wet
And he is my greatest friend when the table is set
Then he sits under the table, you bet
But this is truly mans best friend I have met
He has been close to me since the onset
And should I lose him, I would fret.

Dedicated to Maureen and Austin.

## 469. REFLECTION

Sitting here day after day
Watching the Tulips grow throughout May
Watching the snow fall through December
Time to reflect on the thoughts we remember
Little people running heads covered by scarves and hats
Several items of apparel, which makes them look fat
Sunshine comes and melts the snow
And makes you think how quickly life goes.

Written by Dawn

## 470. SOOTY

I was thinking of getting a kitten to give to someone special
When I was offered one, Sooty being its' title
But when I saw her, black and glossy
Her eyes so green, looking eagerly
I fell in love with her, and her ways
And my children too, want to keep her always.

## 471. FEELINGS: SUFFERING

The will to carry on
You've got to fight to be strong
To give in would be an easy way out
God, if only I could scream and shout
I wait for the day when everything will go away
The memories, the thoughts, the feelings inside
Everything would be easier to sleep forever
Feeling no pain, no suffering whatsoever.

Written by V L

## 472. FEELINGS: MEMORIES

The hurt inside brought tears to her eyes
The thought lingered on in her mind
Trying to find some understanding why
The days, the nights they come and go
Just like her memory, like fading away
She wished she could get away
Get away from everything
But she knows that's an impossible task
And too much to ask.

Written by VL

## 473. BETRAYED

When you're afraid
And you feel betrayed
All you want to do is cry
You ask yourself why
Shall I live or shall I die.

Written by V L

## 474. SLEEP

When you can't sleep
All you do is weep
As you lay the tears fall
Wondering when to end it all.

Written by V L

## 475. INSOMNIA

In bed I lie
Sleep I try
As I toss and turn
My thoughts and feeling begin to burn
The positives and negatives start to flow
Wondering when to sleep I'll go.

Written by V L

## 476. FEELINGS: MOODS

1
The thoughts and feelings begin to flood in
My God what a state I am in
I try to change my thinking pattern
But end up feeling low and flattened
What do I do, I say
Hope and pray they'll go away.

2
Feeling low all week
The solution I try to seek
To help me be stronger and remain in control
But I can't stop the feelings once they're in flow.

Written by V L

## 477. APPETITE

No appetite
No food
I'm not in the mood
No desires
No cravings
Think of all the savings.

Written by V L


## 478. MOTIVATION

I have no motivation at all
I Just stay in and stare at the wall
Don't go out or do anything
What a boring world I live in.

Written by V L


## 479. ARGUING
1.
As they fight, day and night
Arguing and raising voices
Not thinking of others
Sisters and brothers
Their thoughts and feelings at all
When will it all end
Will it ever mend
A message I will send to all
To stop it all.

2.
Shouting and screaming, on and on
All night long
In all this where do I belong
Do I get involved
So it will all be solved
Do I stay out of it all
It's their problem let them deal with it all.

Written by V L




## 480. ILLNESS : DEPRESSION

Depression, Anxiety and stress
It's all a big mess
An illness you can't see
Why me?
I'd rather have a broken arm
That way you could see the harm
It would heal in a short time
You would feel fine
But with me
There's nothing to see
It's all in the mind
A solution I must find.

Written by V L

## 481. SMOKING : HARM

I smoke to relax
What a cost with all the tax
It makes me feel calm
It does me no harm
So what's all this alarm?

Written by V L


## 482. SMOKING: COST

What am I thinking
The cost All this money I've lost
It was once for fun
What have I done.

Written by V L


## 483. LIFE

Full of ups and downs
Why do we frown?
Life is what we make of it
So we try to do better with it.

Written by V L

## 484. UNDERSTANDING

No-one understands you
You want them to
So they can help you
But what do you do?
Live life in despair
Pulling out all your hair
Life can be so unfair.

Written by V L

## 485. PERSONALITY

People change
For good or bad
You may lose what you once had
Your personality changes
From all different ranges.

Written by V L

## 486. PAST

The past catches up with you
That's why you feel the way you do
It plays havoc with your emotions
Wish I had a Magic potion

Written by V L

## 487. REINCARNATION

Life after death I believe
One day I shall leave
Join the spirits above the sky
You're wondering why
It's the way I think and feel
It will help to heal.

As I watch down from above
There is no longer loss of love
The joy of happiness
My life is no longer a distress

Now I am free
I'm so happy as could be
No worries or depression
The tension is lessened.

Written by V L

## 488. CHILDHOOD

Bullying, abuse
Why do others do this to you?
Is it just for fun?
They don't realise what they've done
The harm, the damage
But somehow you try and manage.

Written by V L

## 489. CHILDHOOD II

Childhood can be so cruel
Others use it as a tool
A weapon to hurt you
So young to deal with and understand
Where's the help you seek?
Only yourself and you are weak.

Written by V L




## 490. SCHOOL : FRIENDS

Friendship can be so special
Especially when you're young
But when they hurt and betray you
You cannot forget it at all
Your friends they so call
How could they treat you this way.

Written by V L




## 491. SCHOOL : BULLYING

Fun and games
Then come the names
The bullying begins to start
I feel the fast beats of my heart
I try to hide around the bend
Waiting and hoping for it all to end.

Written by V  L

## 492. SCHOOL : BULLYING

School is supposed to be fun
But soon it can be turned to none
Other kids cause you distress
They make you want to go less and less
Frightened of what they will do next
All I want to do is learn the text
Scared to be alone
They just want to break my bones
At school they roam
I just want to be at home.

Written by V L

## 493. THE SYSTEM

My life they took away
Without any say
No option, no choice
With no voice
The lies, the betrayal
My life they had failed
No understanding, no meaning
They didn't know how I was feeling
Anger and hate
Now it's too late
How will I forget?
They will have no regret.

Written by V L

## 494. FOOD : CRISPS

1.

Crisps come in different shapes and sizes
Some come with great surprises
Free gifts, tokens too
So much for you to choose
Some are round, some are square
Taste the strong ones if you dare.

2.

Crunchy and soft
A whole packet I shall scoff
Different flavours, with great taste
Never let any go to waste
Small packets and large packets
Can you hack it?

Written by V L

## 495. FOOD : CHOCOLATE

1.

Chocolates are black or white
You can eat them day or night
The taste you desire
Your mouth will never tire
You will crave for more
And rush to your nearest store.

2.

Soft and creamy
It will leave you feeling dreamy
The melt in your mouth feeling
Seeing is believing
All the bars you eat
Blimey, you can no longer see your feet.

Written by V L

## 496. T.V. DINNERS / JUNK FOOD

As we sit in front of the telly
The strange noises we hear from our belly
Grumbling, groaning out for food
We just eat our junk food
All that grease, all that fat
We never think of that
The more we eat
That greasy meat
The more we become stuck in our seat.

Written by V L


## 497. FOOD : BISCUITS

The biscuits we dunk
Until off drops a chunk
Soft and soggy they become
As we try to find it with fingers and thumb.

Written by V L


## 498. IRON BRU - DES

He loves his Iron Bru
You should see all the cans he goes through
It's his favourite drink
He's got the Iron Bru link.

Written by V L

## 499. CLEANING - DES

Washing, dusting, hoovering too
He enjoys the jobs except cleaning the loos
Laughing and smiling
He's always happy
In all that he does
He's sure to give you a buzz.

Written by V L


## 500. CUBBY HOLE - DES

Here he sits reading his paper
He is such a caper
Drinking his tea
It's his place to be.

Written by V L

## 501. MARS BARS - FIONA

1.
She'll not be far
Found eating a Mars bar
Her favourite sweet
A Mars bar she cannot defeat.

2.
Mars bars help her work, rest and play
You cannot hide them away
Especially if she's working all day
The chocolate she adores
She'll have you down to the stores
It's her special treat
Which she loves to eat.

3.
Mars bars she would eat
As she relaxed and put up her feet
The silence was golden
Until all had gone
Then came the talking
That didn't take very long.

Written by V L


## 502. THE ASHTRAY

1.
Is used all day long
Creating such a pong
Ash, the ash builds up
Some people want to throw-up
The mess and smell
It's an Ashtray from Hell

2.
An Ashtray is used to rest your butts
People think smokers are nuts
Filled with all that smelly ash
And all that waste of cash
Ashtrays are hard to clean
The bottom can hardly be seen.

Written by V L

### 503. BUBBLE BATH

As the hot water runs
The bubbles begin to form
It looks like frog sporn
The aroma drifts in the room
Just like perfume
The bigger they become
The bath becomes over-run
Bubbles here, bubbles there
They're everywhere.

### 504. THE TELEPHONE

1.
The phone it rings
With good messages it brings
A smile to your face
In every place
Laughter and thrills
Just wait until you get your phone bills

2.
Ring, ring, ring
Deciding if you're out or in
Ring, ring, ring
What messages will it bring
Ring, ring, ring
What a noise, what a din.

Written by V L

## 505. HEALTH

If you've got good health
There's no worries upon yourself
Healthy and fit
You can certainly feel it
Live a happy and prosperous life
Without any worries or strife.

Written by V L

## 506. HURT AND PAIN

1.
Hurt and pain
Things will never be the same
Why should I bother
There is no other
No other, reasons, explanations, why
I no longer want to cry.

2.

I want the pain to heal
To stop how I feel
How does this occur?
I say with a slur
It's all in the mind
Hurting me all the time.

Written by V L


507. VIOLATION

1.

A shock, a horrible surprise
That came to my eyes
I was no longer wise
Although I did try
I didn't know why
It was too late in the end
My body I could not defend.

2.

The body is your own
It should not be overthrown
Protect and defend
The violation, you cannot mend.

Written by V L

## 508. JUSTICE

Where is the justice? I ask
Is it such a hard task?
The decision must be made
Or is it all just a facade
Judges and Lawyers must do their job
Where is the justice?
We have all been robbed.

Written by V L

## 509. MONEY

Notes and coins we receive
But the debts we do not foresee
Money can be financially sound
But leaves us with so little as a pound.

Written by V L

## 510. HOPE

All my hopes were built up
But ended up like an empty cup
What could I have done
All my hopes have gone.

Written by V L

## 512. I DON'T KNOW

Where did the good times go
I don't know
Will they come back
I don't know.

Written by V L

## 513. SADNESS

1.
I'm feeling sad
All that's in me is bad
When I try positive things
All the negatives they bring.

2.
The outlook doesn't appear bright
The falls I've had were not light
So many ups and downs
No wonder I'm always in the mood to frown.

Written by V L

## 514. TRYING

I tried my best
To join the rest
Be independent
Have my own place
But everything blew up in my face.

Written by V L

## 515. RUN AND HIDE

When I'm feeling low
I have nowhere to go
With the feelings inside
I want to run and hide
The hurt cuts so deep
And then I can't even sleep.

Written by V L

## 516. MOVING

Moving was a dream come true
But ended up like having the flu
The headaches, stresses and strains of it all
I just couldn't break down that great big financial wall.

Written by V L

## 517. MOVING

Exhausted and tired
The flat I once desired
Everything seems in tatters
It's all due to money matters.

Written by V L

## 518. MOVING

I had my own reasons to move
I had a lot to prove
To myself and others
Family, friends, Sisters and Brothers
But my reasons were overly judged
Now everythings been smudged
The outlook isn't very clear
I shall try hard not to shed a tear.

Written by V L

## 519. RESPECT

If only I hadn't gone out that day
It would never have been this way
No love, no respect
What did I expect
I can't let go
Even though it hurts
Must try to stop the tears
Before I burst.

Written by V L

## 520. FIGHT

Wash away your tears
Tomorrow will soon be here
Another day, another night
Continue to try and fight.

Written by V L

## 521. FORGET.

Everything's falling apart
Right from the start
That night, never to forget
It was never mean't to be this way
If only I hadn't gone out that day.

Written by V L

## 522. MUSIC I

Music I listen to
Rap, dance, the radio too
The music has different beats
Which makes you jump to your feet
Try to dance on the floor
Out of breath, I can't dance anymore.

Written by V L

## 523. MUSIC II

Loud and fast
Turn it up we'll have a blast
The room begins to shake
All the neighbours I awake
Turn it down, they shout
I wonder what all the fuss is about.

Written by V L

## 524. UNDERSTANDING

No-one understands
They don't really know my fear
They only go off what they hear.

Written by V L

## 525. IT'S OVER

No need to pretend
Our relationship has come to an end
We did not fall out
Had no argument, we did not shout
Can we be friends?
Well that depends
I am willing to enjoy friendship without the loving
But I am afraid that I will always be caring
The latter can't be changed
It is in my nature, and of it I am not ashamed
All I ask is that you speak to me again
My tears no longer pour like rain
I am over the hurt and the sadness
What I want now is only happiness
You introduced me to some lovely people, too
And I will not lose contact with them now, because of you
I see no reason why you should avoid me
There is nothing nicer than a chat over a cup of tea.

## 526. GOING INTO A HOME

Do I need to go into a home?
But would it be like home, with no pets to roam
My family all seem to want me to go
But I am nervous about it, so
I cannot sleep at night
I am all mixed up, and a sight
I want my independence still
I'm not ready to make reality, my will
Once in a small room there
I would not mix with others, or go anywhere
So, I am going to stay where I am, for as long as I can manage
Only then can they parcel me off with all my baggage.


## 527. ALONE

I live on my own
All of my children have from the nest flown
I lost my partner some years passed
And I am awaiting my day, but don't know how long I'll last
For company I keep a pet, or two
If I had my way I'd open up a zoo
Because when I walk into my home
I get a great greeting, so I know that I'm welcome.

## 528. ANOTHER TIME

We lost you, your time was not to be
Now we weep and are drained of energy
Our love is all that keeps us together
But our hearts ache and we feel under the weather
We need a little help to get us through
Sympathy and comfort, and a caring that is true
We will try again to plant a seed
But will never forget you, we have agreed
However we must carry on with our lives and look forward to
future joys
Think of a new bundle and the buying of toys
We will give our love day after day
But will never forget you, in our hearts or as we pray.

## 529. FAITH HEALING

Is the healing for me?
Here is the question but where is the answer?
How I wish I could be made wiser
Is it simply for physical ailments
Or is it for all complaints
Please send a message from beyond to me
So that in it I will both know and see
My mind feels at peace in here
The atmosphere nice, the people sincere
Is this the answer I seek and have had to find
And from here on do I leave my own problems behind
Will this help me to help others?
All my new found Sisters and Brothers
I heal through poetry, art and music
I will bring tranquillity and calmness to the lost and frantic.

## 530. FAITH HEALING II

We sat in chairs, facing each other
Then the healer went through the laying on of hands
My eyes were closed as she gently touched parts of my body
And I felt relaxed and drifted to pleasant lands
Lands where beautiful flowers grew in abundance
And lands where animals roam and dance
When it was all over I opened my eyes
My troubles had lessened and I felt fine for the first time, to
my surprise.


## 531. E.C.T.

I have already explained how E.C.T. was, some ten years ago
It wasn't a pleasant experience, then though
But, now it has been changed for the better
And I feel that that should be expressed in the form of poetry or
letter

E.C.T. is used to raise your mood level
Some people can feel better after a few
Others may need more
But, at the end of the day most have a positive view

Before treatment everyone sits in a waiting room
Where radio music is played softly
Then when your turn comes
You are taken to another room, promptly

On a couch you get, lying down
Then a needle is given, in the back of your hand
The anaesthetic knocks you out
And treatment is given, WHEN YOU are in dreamland

Afterwards, you sit for a while with a cup of tea
Sometimes, you have a bit of a headache, might I mention
And nearly always sleep off the anaesthetic 'till the afternoon
But overall it is no worse than going to the doctors for a blood
test, or injection

A nurse is with you all the time
From the wait beforehand 'till you are taken back to Otterburn or
Delaval
But the treatment is well worthwhile
Because it will help your depression, by lifting your mood level.


## 532. PARANOID THOUGHTS

Why do people always talk about me?
I haven't done anything to them
When I ask them if they have been talking about me
They say "No", but I don't believe them

It happens to me all of the time
And it doesn't seem to matter where I am
I can only cope with it sometimes
They call me, and I am losing my mind, I know I am!

If I come to you and ask
Would you reassure me that I am not
To give me more confidence is myself, is all that I ask
And it would help to know that round the twist I am not!

If necessary would you show me friendship and love
This understanding would help me on my way
Giving a kiss and a cuddle, the love -
Needed from day to day, and is the way

Forward, the way to go from here
I know because, I have been where you are now
And there is a journey, you must travel on to reach this level,
here
But you will receive help, so talk over you troubles, right now.

## 533. I BELIEVE

The heat from your hand
The warmth of your touch
I visit a pleasant land
I am loved so much
A wonderful experience
I look forward to the next time
Once I believed in science
Now, I am writing a rhyme
I believe in God above
I believe in the Spiritual Church
Enjoy life, and send out love
YOU have reached the end of your search.


## 534. HEALING

The healing hand I once believed
Was not for me, and so it seemed
But the truth I learn't recently
Was that the hand was for me too, so deemed
I was afraid to sit in that chair
And I was unsure of what to expect
I did not want to ail anymore
And especially not my mind to infect -
With voices I could not control
But I have now realised that this is not to be
So now I will attend more regularly
Being in control, and totally free.

## 535. LUCK

I now carry on me, notepad and pen
Because I often get the urge to write whether in pub or club
I'm hoping that I don't get that urge when playing my favourite,
bingo
But if someone's going to be lucky, let me know, so that I can get
a rub!


## 536. MATS

Whether clippy mat or proggy mat
We are at it all day long
So if you feel "crafty" and in need of a natter
This is where you belong
You don't need to be bursting with energy
Although we wouldn't mind you bursting into song
We would like your support and company
So, why not come along.

Inspired by Hartley Court, New Hartley.


## 537. COMET

See the comet in the sky
Don't let this opportunity go by
Though it may be cloudy tonight
Through those clouds will shine its' light
Bright, like the North Star
Except its' tail stretches afar
Look out for it this evening
Even through lenses to see it beaming.

## 538. INVENTIONS

Always jumping in and out of cars
And very soon it'll be space shuttles to Mars
But this has made us a lazy lot
And it all started out with the horse, going for a trot
What happened to the good old walk
Nowadays we are all talk
We know what we should do
Was the inventor of the wheel or the like supposed to
Change mankind for the better
It's hard to tell, so I'll lay back on my couch and pick up the
telephone or send a letter!

## 539. A ROSE

A rose is a beautiful flower
Of that there is no doubt
They come in wonderful colours too
Growing from the Spring, and in Summer the blooms open out
But this plant is covered in thorns
All over the woody stems they grow
You don't need to look at it deeply
They are there, all on show
And then there's the briars
Slipping in with their seven leaves
Trying to take over the plant
To take it back to its' wild state, I perceive
Can some people be like a rose?
Full of beauty on the outside
But with a slip in character which is sharp and piercing
With another personality trying to take  over from the inside
A personality which is of the cold state
One which needs to be snipped to be kept in trim
Hidden by beauty, so as to deceive
But if left would be bad to the brim
The bad thoughts, untameable thoughts

Can these thoughts be suppressed?
I believe they can for a time
But then we are again distressed
Some of my bad thoughts are spirits, coming through all at once
causing confusion
And I believe that others' are too
We should try to learn how to control them fully through the
healing process
To be in complete control, as other Mediums practicing do.


## 540. DEADLY NIGHTSHADE

Yet another plant of beauty like the rose
But what lies underneath do you suppose
Poison! Again it is badness
And yet the flowers you would think would offer goodness
Nature is strange
But can be avoided not rearranged
Life is not crazy, everything is there for a reason
Be in control, no more hidden thoughts, be in full bloom only,
this season.


## 541. NONE FOR ME

I have learned the hard way
So now I will always say -
No alcohol for me thank you

The alcohol lowered my mood level, I found
I felt I'd been dragged below ground
No alcohol for me thank you

I ended up in hospital
With suicidal thoughts, and treatment vital
No alcohol for me thank you

Now I say, "None for me"
I would much rather have, orange, coke or cup of tea
No alcohol for me, thank you.


542. JILTED

Jilted, I really feel jilted
Now I know that I'm not wanted
But what keeps me hanging on in there
Is it the love which I hope we can share
One day soon
Stars shine, bright is the moon
What does the future hold is store for me
Keep hanging on in there, wait and see
Too soft by nature I am
And I've landed myself in a jam
The love held back is too great by far
But must be sealed inside this jar.


543. MY PHILOSOPHY

When this you see, remember me
And bear me in your mind
Let all the world, say what they may
Speak of me as you find.

Written by Bill

## 544. A QUIET TIME

We all need some time alone
Some quiet time to call our own
To close our eyes, to close our minds
And leave our material things behind.

Written by Bill


## 545. YOUR PAIN

You are left out in the rain, but you take all of the pain
Just like a soaking rag, your flowering bloom will sag
Yet if they only knew, the pain that you've been through
To a shelter they would run, and pray for healing sun
You can hold your head with pride, you will not be denied
Now you have won the fight, he will guide you to the light.

Written by Bill


## 546. MY DREAM

Out on Safari with rifle in hand
Tracking down game in this glorious land
Is not the life for one such as me
I need to be there forever, wandering and free
Travelling light under deep azure skies
So majestic and perfect to my humble eyes
To be there right now is my lifetime thought
I'm dreaming of Africa, but not for the sport.

## 547. ALONE

What do I feel like sitting alone
The room is full, yet I am still alone
Constant noise, yet it all seems a blur to me
Not one conversation can I follow, it still seems a blur to me
Or should I say a drone
As I can see happy smiling faces, there is still a drone
So, I will continue to sit here, alone
And, I will continue to write, alone
'Till it is time to go home
Not empty, my home
I have my cat to greet me
To have a conversation with her, as her meaiows answer me.

## 548. STONE!

I am not made of stone!
I feel hurt to the bone
I cannot tell you over the phone
And I cannot raise my voice in tone

I hurt deep inside tonight
And I do not know how this can be put right
I went to church hoping to see some light
But I battle on, it's a hell of a fight

Bottling up tears, all day
I never thought I'd feel this way
The love I feel is here to stay
Will time heal? I hope it may.

## 549. SILENCE

I was born into a world of silence
I was born deaf, so I have never heard one single sound
You would think in these wonderful days of science
Some sort of cure would have been found
I find it hard to lip read
As sometimes people don't speak clearly enough
But I sign really well
And I always have a smile, for me that's not so tough
Many people don't make any attempt to talk to me
But that doesn't bother me at all
I like to read and there are things I can do
Like to watch sport, especially football.

Inspired by Leck.


## 550. DISCUSSIONS

Why do men insist on discussing football?
As it never does any good
We all know how they could play
But, it seems, they rarely play the way they should.


## 551. DRUGS

What drugs are on the market?
I honestly don't know
Maybe I'm one of the few
Does my naivety show?
I hear tell that drugs on prescription can be sold on
That's just a rumour I've heard
I would rather not have any drug
But that's something I've always preferred

And yet I've had to have them
I'm on quite a few now
But I intend to come off them
Hopefully without myself and the doctor having a row
My needs have changed
And I intend to sort out my thoughts with the help of the church
So my medication needs to be rearranged
Freedom from drugs, end of my search.


## 552. LONELINESS

All I want is to hear a voice
Your voice is the one I want to hear by choice
Whether in person or over the telephone I hear it
Does not matter because here I always sit
For hours on end I am glued to this chair
That is why I am in despair
So please give me a thought, give me a ring or drop in
I would so much like to know how you've 'bin'.

Inspired by Nora.


## 553. BED

Jumping in and out of bed
What is wrong with your head?
Diseases spread in that way
So why spread your legs, and hope the problem will go away.

## 554. H.I.V.+

Am I H.I.V. positive?
I can't help being negative
It is a hell of a long wait
And I am in one hell of a state!
I cannot concentrate on anything anymore
And think that if I am, how will I even up the score
I am passed crying, no tears to pour
Yet, I thought I'd have enough to fill the seashore.

## 555. HISTORY LESSON

A Dutchman called Prince William
And an Englishman - King James
Fell out and started feuding
And called each other names

T'was for the throne of England
But for reasons not quite clear
They came across to Ireland
To do their fighting here

They had Sarsfield, they had Shomberg
They had horse and foot and guns
And they landed up at Carrick
With a thousand Lambeg drums

They had lots of Dutch and Frenchmen
And battalions and platoons
Of Russians and of Prussians
And Bulgarian dragoons

And they politely asked the Irish
If they'd kindly like to join
And the whole affair was settled
At the battle of the Boyne

Then William went to London
And James went off to France
And the whole kibosh left Ireland
Without a backward glance

And the poor abandoned Irish
Said "Good-bye" to Kind and Prince
And went on with the fighting
We've been at it ever since.

Anon.


## 556. PROOF

This I do not need
This I have already had
In a garden I am the strongest weed
The thistle, and of it I am glad

Gather around if proof is what YOU need
Church can provide this as already planted is the seed
Spread the word amongst the crowd
And the result will make you feel proud.


## 557. DIANA

Those who have looked to me in admiration
Now stand together as one congregation
In such a short life
I have seen much pain and strife
Talked with the terminally ill
To find both courage and happiness still
My own time has come, and gone
May the nation reflect upon what has been done
Then may it carry on
As one.